PREPARING MUSIC MANUSCRIPT

PREPARING

PRENTICE-HALL, INC.   ENGLEWOOD CLIFFS, NEW JERSEY

MUSIC MANUSCRIPT

ANTHONY DONATO—PROFESSOR OF THEORY AND COMPOSITION— SCHOOL OF MUSIC—NORTHWESTERN UNIVERSITY

PRENTICE-HALL INTERNATIONAL, INC., LONDON
PRENTICE-HALL OF AUSTRALIA, PTY., LTD., SYDNEY
PRENTICE-HALL OF CANADA, LTD., TORONTO
PRENTICE-HALL OF INDIA (PRIVATE) LTD., NEW DELHI
PRENTICE-HALL OF JAPAN, INC., TOKYO
PRENTICE-HALL DE MEXICO, S.A., MEXICO CITY

PREPARING MUSIC MANUSCRIPT by Anthony Donato

Second printing......

Library of Congress Catalog Card Number 63-16352

Printed in the United States of America   28758 c

PREFACE

THE WRITING of this guide book is the result of constantly recurring questions from students in regard to the proper procedure for the preparation and copying of music manuscript.

As every teacher of composition, theory, orchestration, or any other course requiring the notation of music is too well aware, endless time is consumed in explaining the fundamentals of note placement and general music calligraphy in all its technical aspects. This is only natural, since most students give little thought to printed symbols representing musical ideas and take for granted the form in which they are presented.

It is assumed that anyone using this guide will be familiar with elementary musical principles. It should also be understood that the guide deals only with notation and layout procedures and is not intended to be a method or course in copying. Elementary notation, theory, orchestration, and other technical factors are mentioned in the text only when it is necessary to clear up a point pertaining to writing of music manuscript.

The instructions and models given are all based on generally accepted commercial engraving and autograph practices as used by leading publishers. Any deviation from such practice is clearly indicated and is given as an optional procedure.

Most of the comments apply equally to manuscript made with either hand pens or by music typewriter.

A.D.

TABLE OF CONTENTS

PREPARING MUSIC MANUSCRIPT

1

THE CASE FOR CLARITY

COPYING MUSIC is a phase of musical activity that concerns everyone connected with the art. All students must copy numerous theory, counterpoint, and other examples almost from their first days of study, and many of them are concerned with the copying of orchestral or band scores and parts, which they have arranged as a part of their routine training. For composers, copying is as essential as learning the fundamentals of music. Even those established composers who give most of their copy work to professional copyists usually prepare their own scores in order to be absolutely certain that everything is in order. There is also the fact that, with costs of preparation of manuscripts for publication constantly going up, many composers are making their own publication copies to be printed in manuscript facsimile.

Making beautiful manuscript is an art that is mastered only with great care and considerable effort. As in performance, some people are more gifted for it than others and will turn out better work, but anyone with a knowledge of music and with normal control of his muscular facilities is capable of producing correct and reasonably legible manuscript with a bit of care and practice.

The importance of producing good manuscript cannot be over-estimated. A fine, well-prepared score or part immediately receives better attention from any reader. This fact is extremely important to composers submitting works to conductors, performers, or contests. No matter how objective a reader may try to be, a fine score is bound to make a better impression simply by being more attractive in appearance and easier to read. Without a doubt, many a contest or performance has been lost because of an unattractive manuscript.

Performers, conductors, and judges of contests are far too often asked to read scores and parts that can only be considered disgraceful. The player in a professional orchestra has no choice and must bear with what is set before him, but many solo and ensemble players refuse to work with bad scores and parts, and rightly so. As for conductors, they have every right to refuse to read an illegible score, and they often do. Composers, both professional and student, who solicit performances either from friends or from strangers, should consider it mandatory—an act of courtesy—to supply the best manuscripts possible.

In addition to being attractive in appearance, a music manuscript must be correct in its technical details. The principles of music notation are so standardized that there is negligible variation the world over. In spite of this fact many manuscripts look as though the writers had had no contact with music fundamentals. In some cases this is due to carelessness; in others it is due to musical illiteracy; and in still others it is a lackadaisical "make-do" attitude. In no case may the result be condoned.

Near perfection, such as that found in the finest engraving or autographing, is an ideal seldom attained, but it may always serve as a standard of measurement. Most free-hand music manuscript will be far from perfect at its best, but every copyist should strive for the greatest clarity and attractiveness compatible with a reasonable rate of copying speed. Very few persons have either the time or the inclination to produce manuscript by autograph methods—carefully ruling all note stems and beams and resorting to guide lines and other aids. Such care is usually reserved for preparation for publication. This, however, need not be considered a liability in practical terms. Handwritten music manuscript, like ordinary penmanship, can have beauty under its own terms, showing the personal characteristics of the copyist, and, with care in regard to the technical details, convey the thought of the musical content with complete satisfaction.

For those who have the inclination or the need to duplicate the appearance of the best published music in their copying, it will be necessary to use either autography or music typewriter methods. In any event, whether the work is produced by free-hand method, by autography, or by music typewriter, the technical requirements for the content must be identical, with the same goal in view, namely, to convey accurately on paper a musical idea to a performer or to a reader.

2

THE COPYIST'S EQUIPMENT

A S WE STATED in Chapter 1, making beautiful (or even acceptable) manuscript is an art that is mastered only with great care and considerable effort. Any time spent in assembling suitable materials will far more than repay itself in both speed of operation and quality of work produced.

The materials listed here are all readily available. Not all of them are essential; on the other hand, some copyists will want additional items not mentioned. The list is intended to serve as a suggestion to those who may be at a loss as to where to begin. With a little experience the new copyist will determine just what suits his particular needs and tastes. He can then make substitutions, additions, or deletions accordingly.

The larger the number of mechanical aids used for making music manuscript, the nearer the result comes to what is known as *autograph*, a carefully controlled and guided system of manuscript production widely used for commercial reproduction.

Paper. There is a wide choice of papers available in sizes and formats for nearly every purpose in both opaque and transparent types. The copyist should try to examine the same size sheet in various makes, since there are considerable differences in color shades, in space between staves, and in staff line separation. Bear in mind that opaque paper on which ink is to be used should be of firm texture; soft paper will cause feathering of the ink. Transparent papers all have very hard surfaces, but they vary considerably in abrasive resistance and in density.

Sheet sizes and recommended rulings for particular combinations will be discussed in the chapters on specific procedures for various solo and ensemble needs.

Ink. Any ink used for music manuscript should be black. This means a true black, not blue-black. Colored inks are not acceptable.

On opaque manuscript paper not intended for reproduction any good black ink will do. Transparencies (onion skin) for reproduction require a heavy ink which makes consistently opaque characters without variation. Most fountain pen inks are too light in texture for good reproduction, because the light characters such as note stems are not as opaque as note heads. Since most people prefer the convenience of working with a fountain pen, the problem arises of getting a heavy ink that will flow fairly well. *Higgins Engrossing Ink* seems to solve this problem quite well. This ink flows in a fountain pen with a music point, and it makes all characters uniformly black—from fine note stems to heavy rests. When using this ink, it is necessary to wash out the pen at fairly frequent intervals in order to avoid clogging the feeding system.

Higgins Eternal Ink, sometimes recommended, is not very satisfactory because of the fact that it dries with a slight powdery deposit which is apt to smear over any pages that come into contact with it. Drawing ink of the kind used by draftsmen cannot be used in a fountain pen but can be used for hand-dipped pens with excellent results.

There are several inks on the market made especially for music writing. Some of these are of the consistency of regular fountain pen ink and manuscript made with them will not reproduce well. The heavier music writing inks such as *Monarch* and *Cameo* are similar to Engrossing ink. These produce consistently opaque characters which will give fine reproduction from onion skins. These, too, will flow in a fountain pen, but one must expect faster pen clogging from them than from regular fountain pen inks. Frequent rinsing helps to prolong the periods of use before cleaning is necessary.

Pens. The choice of pen points depends in part on personal preference and in part on the type of manuscript to be written. One will find a large selection of points suitable for music writing for both dip pens and fountain pens. There are special points for music writing which have two and three points, or nibs, available in varying degrees of breadth and flexibility. If it is at all possible, one should experiment with different types, keeping in mind that no single point can possibly take care of all contingencies. One should also be aware of the fact that any point will produce heavier characters with heavy ink than with ordinary fountain pen ink.

If one were to be limited to only one three-pronged point, the most useful choice would be a fine point. The next addition would be a three-prong medium point. These points are best for the pressure system of writing, producing well-shaped note heads, and spreading readily for the wide beams of grouped notes. Music points are manufactured by several American and European firms and are available for purchase at music stores and at special pen shops.

Many copyists find that their needs are fully satisfied with ordinary writing points. The *Esterbrook* fountain pen, made for instant exchange of points, is very popular; the points are relatively inexpensive, and the instant change of points permits of some experimentation before purchase.

One of the most valuable aids for making neat manuscript is a draftsman's ruling pen. For drawing bar lines and other straight lines it is almost indispensable, since the lines drawn with such a pen are absolutely uniform in width and density. Line width is adjustable by a small thumbscrew and can be varied from that of a hair-line to one of nearly one eighth of an inch. The pen must be hand-filled with a quill such as that on the stopper of a drawing-ink bottle.

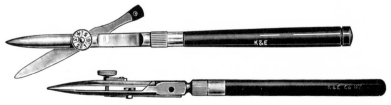

Ruling pens

One will also need several steel points for lettering of texts and performance indications. Most of this work can be done with fine and medium points. For heavy lettering such as that used for title pages, there is a very useful type of point known as a *Speed Ball*. This is available in various degrees of breadth with both round and straight tips, giving a choice of lines with rounded or squared termination.

The following list of pen points, given in graduated order from fine to heavy, should take care of most lettering needs.

Gillotts No. 70
Spencerian No. 1
Gillotts No. 303
Esterbrook Falcon No. 048
Hunt Speedball No. B - 3
Hunt Speedball No. B - 5

Pen Cleaning Materials. Pen points must always be clean to insure free flow of ink. Heavy ink gradually builds up a deposit on the metal which will corrode steel pens. A dirty point will also cause characters to be thicker and heavier than those made with a clean point. Pen wipers and blotters should be used frequently on the points. We should note here that blotters must never be used to take up ink on work being done, except in case of error. (See the section on correcting mistakes.) Inked characters must be left to dry naturally in order to remain dark. This is especially important on transparent papers, because faint characters do not reproduce well.

The ink sacs in fountain pens need occasional rinsing with water. Some copyists, when using heavy ink, empty and rinse their pens after each period of use. Despite the best of care, however, heavy ink will clog the feed system of fountain pens in time. Sometimes, though, a pen that seems hopelessly clogged can be restored to use by immersing the tip and the lower barrel in a special solvent, such as *Higgins Pen Cleaner*. These solvents are also good for cleaning corroded or caked points.

Rulers. A good ruler (or straight edge) is indispensable. A metal ruler with a cork or rubber back is to be preferred; this non-skid feature will save many freshly-inked pages from being smeared. Metal rulers are available in various lengths, the fifteen-inch being a convenient length that will take care of most assignments. Whatever the type of ruler used, it must have a raised edge to avoid blotting the ink, unless it is being used exclusively with a ruling pen. Metal is better than plastic, because the edge will remain smooth longer.

In addition to serving as a straight edge for ruling lines, a ruler provides a simple and quick means for marking measures of equal size. For example, let us assume that on a page with staves eight inches in width, the problem is to find equidistant points for marking off five measures with the first measure sufficiently larger to accommodate a clef sign and key and meter signatures. An arbitrary linear value per measure is selected, the only requirement being that the total distance on the ruler must be greater than the width of a staff line. In this case, two inches per measure is a convenient figure, since the total for the five measures is ten inches. The starting end of the ruler is placed near the beginning of a staff line at the bottom of the page, allowing sufficient space for a clef sign and key and meter signatures. The other end is pivoted about this point until the ten-inch mark falls on a staff line. With the ruler angled on the page, points are marked at the two-, four-, six-, and eight-inch marks, and measure lines are ruled from these points, at right angles to the staves.

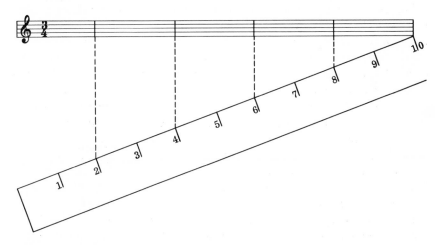

Making measures with rulers

Correcting Mistakes. Mistakes are inevitable, even under the best of conditions. For erasing ink, a soft rubber eraser of the kind used for mechanical and architectural drawing will do a cleaner job than the hard rubber kind usually sold for an ink eraser. The paper-wrapped erasers in pencil form are convenient in tight places. In erasing ink, the best results with any eraser are obtained by rubbing lightly, without trying to hurry the result. Frequently brushing away the residue also helps.

An erasing shield is helpful in confining the erasure to a limited area.

A sharp penknife or razor blade may be used for scratching out mistakes that do not lend themselves to easy erasure. On opaque paper, ink applied to scraped surfaces is apt to feather; to avoid this, it is best to make the necessary corrections first, scratching out the mistakes after the ink is thoroughly dry. Admittedly, this corrective procedure is not always very successful, but it is usually satisfactory for minor errors.

Extensive erasures can be made with much less effort by using an *erasing machine,* an electrically-powered device which has a small, rapidly-revolving abrasive tip.

For larger areas it is advisable to splice (or strip) in a new area of clean paper. On opaque paper the simplest method of doing this is to paste a remedial strip over the bad part. The most satisfactory adhesive to use for this purpose is rubber cement. It is easy to use, dries fast and does not curl the paper. Any residue is easily removed by rubbing it off with a clean finger-tip or with a cement eraser, made for this purpose. Needless to say, the paper used for the patch should be of the same type as that of the original sheet.

Mistakes on transparencies can be corrected in the same manner, except that pasting patches over mistakes in transparencies is not possible because of the increased opacity, which shows up in reproduction as a dark area. Most transparent music paper today has the staves printed on the *back* of the sheet, making it possible to erase without damaging the staff lines. Sometimes small mistakes which are not on a staff can be excised by cutting out the bad part with a knife or razor blade. Where errors cover a large area it is better to cut off a complete portion of a sheet and attach a similar part of a new one, or to splice in a new segment equal in size to the cut-out portion. In either case, the new segments must be fastened to the old sheet with gummed tape, *Scotch Tape No. 810* being excellent for this purpose, because it will not affect reproduction of the work.

Erasures on any kind of paper are made easier if the mistake is noticed immediately and lightened with a blotter. This, incidentally, is the only condition under which a blotter should be applied directly to work being done.

Attempts to erase excessively large areas are a waste of time. In correcting large mistakes, if splicing as described above is not feasible, it is best to do the entire page over. Usually this is actually faster than the effort expended in erasure or delicate scratching, and the result is far better.

Lettering Devices. Performance indications, titles, vocal texts, and other directions or information requiring a degree of uniformity will be much neater if the lettering and spacing is done with some mechanical aid.

The most common and most readily available aid to uniform lettering is an ordinary typewriter. This can be extremely useful for the printing of performance directions, texts of vocal music, and various other information. Carriages of standard typewriters will take a music page of eleven by fourteen inches in size and will permit typing almost to the page-edge limits. Wider carriages are available if needed for work on larger pages.

For free-hand lettering one of the most useful devices is the *Braddock-Rowe Lettering Triangle,* available in shops that sell draftsmen's supplies. With this triangle, guide lines for limiting letter sizes can be drawn swiftly and accurately in spacings varying from one thirty-second of an inch to two inches. The triangle also has a slot for drawing inclined guide lines to aid in drawing slanted letters. In conjunction with a ruler, the side of the triangle may be used for drawing vertical guide lines for vertical letters.

Use of the triangle for drawing limit lines for letters is quite simple. As seen in the illustration below, there are several sets of small holes just large enough to accept a well-sharpened pencil point, which are drilled at varying distances. By placing a pencil point in one of the holes and drawing the pencil, with the triangle, along the edge of a ruler and then repeating the operation with another hole selected at the desired distance from the first hole, one will have two or more perfectly spaced parallel guide lines. These should be drawn very lightly and erased after the desired ink lettering is thoroughly dry.

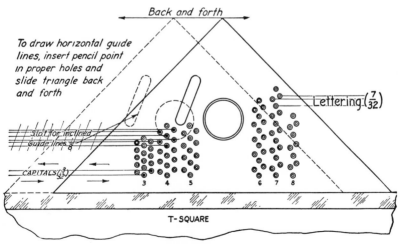

Warren J. Luzadder, *Fundamentals of Engineering Drawing,* 4th Ed., © 1959 by Prentice-Hall, Inc. Englewood Cliffs, N.J. by permission.

Lettering triangle

A widely-used aid for uniform lettering is the *Leroy Lettering Instrument*. A special point, or stylus, follows grooved letters in a guide, while an inking point moves simultaneously on the paper being lettered. Templates and pens for various sizes and styles may be changed as needed. There is an arm on the instrument that is adjustable to make either vertical or oblique (inclined) letters.

Courtesy Keuffel & Esser Co.

Leroy lettering instrument

Templates for the most commonly used music symbols are also available for use with this device. Such mechanical aids are indispensable for autography.

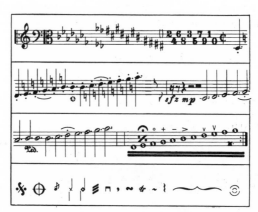

Courtesy Keuffel & Esser Co.

Leroy music template

Another aid for printing larger letters is a *Lettering Guide*. These guides, made of metal or plastic, are available for letters and numerals of various sizes and styles can be used with or without a special lettering pen designed for them.

AI3CDEGHJKLMN0P..STUVWXYZ 234567•°9&abcdefghijkmnopqr-stuvwxyz
◆   AI3CDEGHJKLMN0P..STUVWXYZ234567•°9&   ★
AI3CDEGHJKLMN0P..STUVWXYZ234567•°9&

Lettering guide

Rubber stamp letter sets, available in several sizes and styles, and stamp sets containing names of instruments, in various sizes, are easy to use and provide a simple method for obtaining uniform lettering.

One of the simplest methods for obtaining uniform lettering is by use of acetate or friction transfer letters. These come in sheets of letters and figures in numerous sizes and styles. Sheets containing miscellaneous symbols and music symbols are also available. These may be obtained from stores carrying artist's or draftsmen's materials. They are made under various trade names—Artype, Craftype, Tecnifax, and Letraset being some of the best-known. Letraset is especially convenient to use, each character transferring directly from the sheet without the need for cutting out the desired symbol. Characters of this type may be used on any kind of paper, including transparent sheets.

Curves. A draftsman's *irregular curve* or a *French curve* will help in drawing slurs that are too long to be done neatly in freehand strokes. When using these devices with ink, it is essential to use a ruling pen, since the edges of these plastic instruments are not raised, and an ordinary pen will cause smearing of the ink.

Courtesy Keuffel & Esser Co.

Curves

The *flexible curve,* a newer device for drawing curves, is made with a soft metal core surrounded by a spring, to which is attached a flat metal strip serving as a guide for a pen or pencil. Any kind of pen may be used without smearing. This curve is probably easier to use than the two mentioned above. It comes in several lengths, the twelve-inch curve being sufficient for most musical needs.

Flexible curve

Dividers and Compasses. A set of dividers can be a great help for rapidly estimating measure distances if all the measures of a page are equidistant. When using dividers to divide a staff into equal parts, a trial and error system is used. Adjust the dividers, with the fingers of the hand holding them, to the approximate size of the desired measure. Place one point of the dividers at the right end of the staff line and then rotate the dividers through 180 degrees from one side to the other, stepping off the distance of the estimated measure until the beginning of the staff line has been reached. If the estimate for the first measure of the staff is too large and the last measure too short, decrease the divider spread proportionately and repeat the operation. With a little practice one will acquire the knack for judging the distance of the first measure with surprising accuracy.

Measurement need not be excessively critical, since it is desirable to have the last measure stepped off (the actual first measure on the staff) slightly longer than the others in order to allow space for the clef sign and possibly a key signature and/or a meter signature. The

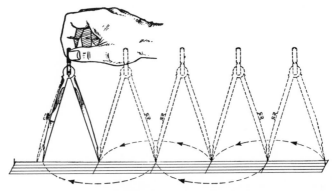

Stepping off measures with dividers

use of this system to determine the spacing of equidistant measures can save much time that might be used in measuring with a ruler, especially where several successive pages have the same measure ruling.

A compass is sometimes used for drawing long slurs. For this purpose a compass of considerable expansion is necessary in order to obtain a broad arc to produce a flat, rather than highly, arched slur.

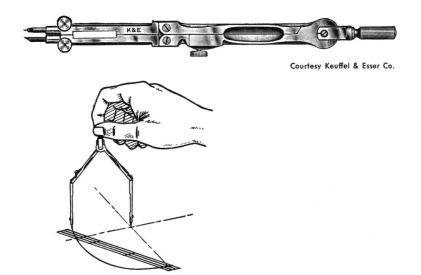

Courtesy Keuffel & Esser Co.

Warren J. Luzadder, *Fundamentals of Engineering Drawing*, 4th Ed., © 1959 by Prentice-Hall, Inc. Englewood Cliffs, N.J. by permission.

Drawing slur with compass

Music Typewriters. Although music typewriters have had limited use in the past, it is only in recent years that they have been developed to the extent of attracting users in considerable numbers. Publishers are using them for preparation of material for photoengraving and many composers, arrangers. and copyists have them for their own use.

A music typewriter such as the *Musicwriter,* one of the best-known, can produce excellent work by a person who has learned to use it. As with a regular typewriter, one must put in a reasonable amount of time in practice before attempting any final copy. Properly used, a type-writer can produce work ready for reproduction except for long slurs, titles, and a few directions. A skilled operator moves at a fair rate of speed, although not at one to equal that of a good copyist. The work, however, will have an appearance close to that of engraving. Everything considered, the music typewriter is a very valuable addition to the resources available for the reproduction of music.

Very slowly (♩ = 56)

3

GENERAL NOTATION

THE PROPER PLACEMENT of notes on a staff, along with various directions for performance, is one of the most important requirements not only for neat and attractive manuscript but also for insuring the accurate conveyance of a musical idea. The discussion of this chapter is concerned mainly with the problems of calligraphy, since it is assumed that the reader has a knowledge of music fundamentals. Furthermore, the material of this section is of a nature pertaining to all types of music. Special problems, notation, and symbols encountered in specific categories will be discussed in the next chapter.

Bar Lines, Braces and Brackets. Bar lines are used to connect staves at the beginning and end of score lines and to mark off measures. Single staff music, such as parts for single line instruments, does not have a bar line at the beginning of the staff. The lines should be approximately twice the width of note stems. Heavier lines that are used for brackets, repeat signs and double bars at the end of works should be just slightly wider than one-half the width of a space between two staff lines.

In addition to bar lines, braces are used (a) to connect the staves of score lines for two-staff instruments, such as harp and piano and (b) to mark off like instruments in ensemble music.

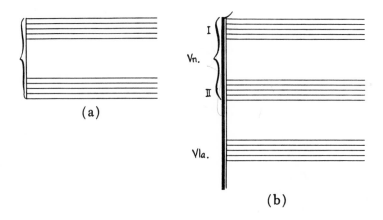

Brackets are used (a) to connect the staves of complete scores, sections, or choirs in both instrumental and vocal music and (b) to connect the staves of like instruments. In the latter instance, a second bracket is used in addition to the choir bracket, in place of a brace as in example (b) immediately above.

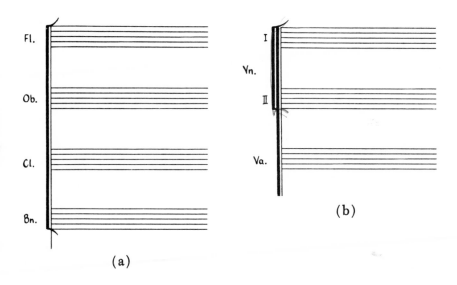

(a)

(b)

Clef Signs. There seems to be considerable variation in handwritten characters for the various clef signs and coypists develop personal touches over a period of time. However, particularly for the beginner, one cannot err by imitating the printed characters found in good editions of well-known publishers. In making characters by hand slight deviations necessarily occur, and the copyist will soon develop his own style.

The clefs shown below are the ones in common use today as seen in engraved music.

The treble clef sign has as its focal point the note G on the second line from the bottom of the staff; the bass clef sign point is the fourth line F; and the central point of the alto and tenor clefs is always middle C.

Clef signs are normally placed on a staff as shown above. There is, however, a new version of the treble clef sign that is sometimes used to show the treble clef on several adjacent staves in ensemble music as shown in the following example.

Key and Meter Signatures. Sharps and flats for key signatures must be placed on the correct lines or spaces. In contemporary music key signatures are usually omitted, accidentals being placed on the staff directly in front of a note as needed.

All key signatures, as they appear in treble, alto, tenor, and bass clefs, are shown in the table on page 23.

Meter (time) signatures are placed directly following a key signature if there is one; otherwise immediately after the clef sign.

On a single staff the numerals are placed within the limits of the outer staff lines. In chamber, orchestra, band, and other music for large ensembles one will often see an enlarged signature serving several staves in order to make it easier to read the meter changes in the score.

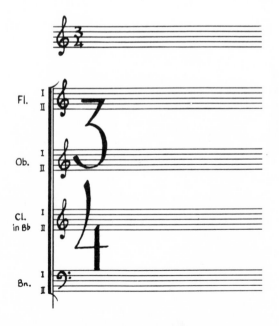

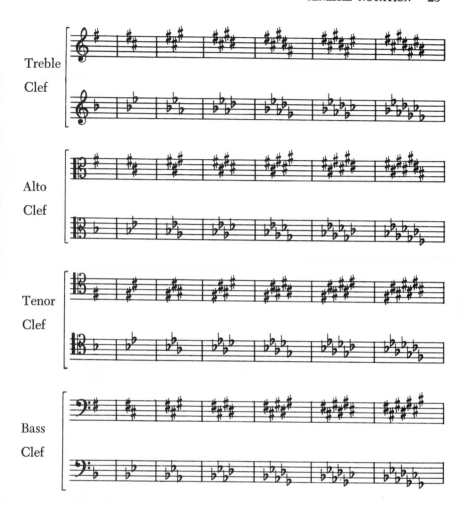

There are two new methods for showing meters and unit values. They are shown in the following example, along with their corresponding standard equivalents.

Note Heads. Note heads should be of a size to fit snugly within the confines of the space between two lines of the printed staves of the paper being used. When placed on a line, the note heads must be of the same size as those within a space, and centered. Careless centering will create confusion in reading. Uniformity of size is important, because note heads that are too large or too small, aside from their poor appearance, can often raise a doubt as to their exact pitch intent.

In shape, the note heads should be very broad or round ovals and inclined toward the right. If the note heads are to be made with the pressure system, using a flexible point, one must be careful to hold the pen in such a manner that the resulting heads slant to the right. Note heads made this way are apt to be less uniform than those that are drawn, but it is a very popular method for producing fast copy, and with practice the results can be not only satisfactory but also very attractive.

Poor   Good

Cue notes and ornamental (grace) notes should be much smaller than the regular notes, but they should be consistent in size, properly centered, and slanted to the right.

Poor   Good

Time Dots. A dot that is used to increase the durational value of a note by one-half its original value is placed in the same space as that of the note. If the note is on a line, the dot is placed in the space immediately above.

Two dots, which increase the original note value by one-half plus one-quarter, are placed in the same relative position as the single dot.

Leger Lines. Accuracy and ease of reading will be assured only if leger lines are carefully placed. They must have the same spacing distances as the lines of the printed staff to which they are added. Nothing can be more frustrating and irritating to a performer than having to read a series of consecutive leger-lined notes that are inaccurately placed. Whether done by free-hand methods or with guide lines, with reasonable care and practice the problem of spacing leger lines can be solved successfully. The difference in neatness and in ease of reading will be apparent by comparing the two notations in the example that follows.

Poor   Good

Stems. For single notes, stems extending downward are placed on the left side of the note head; stems extending upward are placed on the right side. The length of the stem for a single note is approximately the distance of the width of three staff spaces. Multiple-note chords, naturally, will require stems sufficiently longer to accommodate the additional distance created by the larger number of notes. Stems should be drawn as thin lines and should touch the note heads.

The middle of a staff is used as the guide point to determine the direction in which a note stem should extend from the note head. In most cases, notes on or above the middle line are given stems extending downward from the left side of the note head, whereas the notes below this line are given stems extending upward from the right side of the note head.

Exceptions to this practice will be encountered in groups of beamed notes; the reason for this is explained in the section pertaining to beams.

The stemming of notes to be sounded simultaneously is done on the same principle as that for single notes, with one exception. Seconds, being only one staff degree apart and therefore very closely spaced, need to be written with a note head on either side of the stem. The note heads are placed on the staff in ascending pitch order.

Observe that the stem for a second is always placed on the right side of the note head of lower pitch, regardless of the direction in which the stem is turned.

For simultaneously sounding pitches of three or more notes the same point of reference, the middle staff line, is used for stem placing. Stems of chords or clusters that are predominantly below the middle line are extended upward; stems for note groupings predominantly in the upper portion of the staff are extended downward.

Multiple note groupings involving seconds will necessitate note heads on both sides of the stem, just as for two notes. Note heads are placed according to ascending pitch order, with as many note heads as possible on the correct side of the stem.

In ambiguous cases, where the stem might go in either direction, point the stem downward.

Stems extending both upward and downward from the same note heads are occasionally needed to show differing time values occurring in two different voices on the same pitch or for indicating a unison in two different voices.

Such notation, of course, is not possible if one of the voices of common pitch is a half-note or a whole-note of time value and different from the value of the other voice. One note head cannot be both black and white at the same time, and in the case of whole- and half-notes, a stem would cancel out the whole-note value.

If more than one independent part is written on a single staff, it is sometimes desirable or even necessary to show voice separation by pointing all the stems for one part in the same direction.

There are two methods for stemming cue notes. In the first, the cue notes are written with small heads and with stems placed in the usual manner with reference to the middle line dividing point of the staff. Rests for the principal voice may or may not be used. The name of the instrument playing the notes cued is placed at the beginning of the cued notes.

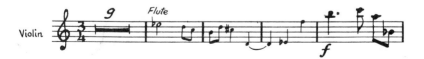

In the second method of notation, stems all run in the same direction regardless of note placement on the staff. Full-sized rests are placed for the principal voice either at the top or bottom of the staff rather than in the center. The name of the instrument playing the cue is placed as in the first method.

The second method of notation in the example above seems to be the clearest and easiest to read and is the one most often used.

Stems for ornamental (grace) notes are pointed upward, without exception.

Flags (hooks). The flags for single eighth-, sixteenth-, and smaller-value notes are always placed on the right side of the note stem regardless of stem direction. The flags are added to note stems of normal length, curving inward toward the stems, ending just short of the note heads. Each additional flag added to a stem requires that the stem be longer by the distance of one space of the staff.

The flag for a single grace note has a line drawn through it, passing through the note stem.

Beams. In all instrumental music most notes of less than quarter-note duration are linked together with beams. The same notation practices are often now applied to vocal music. Beams as used in the traditional method of vocal notation will be discussed in the section on vocal music in Chapter 4.

Beams should be approximately the width of one-half the space between two staff lines. The space between two beams should be slightly less than the width of a beam.

In general, stemming practices as applied to single notes prevail for notes connected by beams, the objective being the placement of a majority of the stems in a given grouping in the right direction.

At times, in order to preserve balance, a single note farthest removed from the middle staff line will determine the stem directions, causing the remaining stems in the group to point in what would normally be the wrong direction.

The slant of a beam follows the contour or progress of a majority of the notes in the beamed group.

Figures beginning and ending with the same notes have horizontal beams.

Prime consideration must be given to maintaining clear unit division. Simple unit meters demand different beaming procedures from those of compound meters, and in both simple and compound triple meters beaming differs from that of duple and quadruple.

The regular divisions of the most commonly used time units are given in Table 1. Beaming practices are based on variations or combinations of these basic divisions.

Table 1   Note Value Divisions

Occasionally it is permissible to beam notes of like value which exceed the value of a single time unit.

Note that in the third measure the three eighth-notes are beamed together but in the fourth measure the first eighth-note is detached from the two that follow it in order to retain clear identity of the unit divisions.

The notes of the example above would be perfectly correct in $\frac{2}{4}$ meter, except for the fourth measure, which would be altered as below.

Under normal conditions in quadruple meter, divisions of more than two units are not beamed unless an unusual accent or phrasing situation demands otherwise.

Occasionally   Preferred

Notes of the value of a sixteenth or less should always be grouped to show a well-defined unit. In the following example in $\frac{4}{4}$ meter the divisions of the unit into four sixteenth-notes are best separated, although one occasionally sees eight sixteenths beamed together in order to emphasize smoothness of execution.

Occasionally   Preferred

Occasionally   Preferred

Figures resulting from dividing a unit into eight parts are clearer if subdivision is shown by using beams of unequal length.

Some of the incorrect notation of the foregoing examples becomes correct in triple meter. The six beamed eighth-notes of the second measure of the following example are correct and represent normal notation for such a division in triple meter. Observe, however, that the three eighth-notes of the fourth measure are not beamed together; the separation of the first eighth-note from the two following assures the retention of the identity of the simple unit of the triple meter.

Beamed groups of three and six notes are correct in compound meters. Note also, in the following example, that the first two sixteenth-notes of the second measure are not connected to the six that follow. This separation is necessary to preserve the distinct unit division.

Grace notes, when beamed, are usually given sixteenth-note values for two notes beamed together and thirty-second-note values for groups of four or more.

When notes of differing values of less than quarter-note duration are linked together with beams, a short beam is placed on the right side of the note stem if the short note is the first note in the beamed group. All other short beams in the group are placed on the left sides of note stems.

Beamed figures involving dotted notes will also need short beams for the short note values. If a short note occurs at the start of a beamed group, the short beam is placed on the right side of the note stem. Beams for all succeeding short notes are placed on the left sides of the note stems.

Deviations from the normal beaming of notes are sometimes made in order to emphasize phrasing or changed accentuation due to unusual note grouping.

(a)

(b)

There are mixed feelings about the extension of beams over bar lines as seen in the second line of the example above, but such note groupings are found frequently in contemporary music.

Incomplete beaming of a regular note group is sometimes used to show a sudden change of dynamics.

The same procedure may be used to emphasize contrapuntal design or phrasing.

(a)

(b)

Accessory Numerals. Any metric division that is a departure from normal division of a unit or a combination of units is indicated by a small numeral placed above or below the note group. In this category are duplets, triplets, quadruplets, and any other abnormal divisions of a unit of a measure, as well as such divisions or figures of equal note values that extend over the time space of more than a single unit and do not conform to exact measured values.

The practice of enclosing these numerals with a small slur or bracket is no longer followed except in those cases where there might be some doubt about the note grouping. Where the notes are connected with beams and where mixed note value figures are clear, a numeral by itself is sufficient. The numeral is placed over or under beams and stems, except where such a placement would cause crowding, in which case it is placed over or under note heads. Eliminating the small slurs gives the music a cleaner look and placing the numerals over or under the stems has the advantage of keeping the note heads free for legato and other slurs.

Where a regular succession of such figures is made perfectly evident by the notation of the note groupings, it is not necessary to repeat the numeral for each grouping, one or two at the start of the series being sufficient.

Where note groupings cover a larger span it is necessary to use a bracket or a slur. The preference today is for a bracket, partly because it cannot be confused with a legato or bowing slur. The bracket is placed over or under note stems wherever possible. Where note stems of the figure extend in both directions the bracket is placed above the staff.

Where dynamics might cause crowding it is best to place the brackets on the opposite side of the staff.

Accessory numerals indicate a reduction of true note values except in the case of figures resulting from dividing dotted time units into duplets or quadruplets and using the numerals as substitutes for time dots. In such instances the notes of division are actually increased in value.

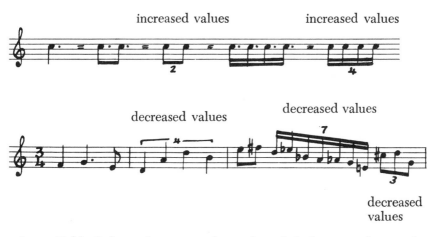

Rests. Table 2 shows the commonly used symbols for rests along with equivalent note values.

Table 2

SIMPLE NOTATION

American Name	British Name	Rest Symbol	Note Value
Double Whole	Breve		
Whole	Semibreve		
Half	Minim		
Quarter	Crotchet		
Eighth	Quaver		
Sixteenth	Semiquaver		
Thirty-second	Demisemiquaver		
Sixty-Fourth	Hemidemisemiquaver		

COMPOUND NOTATION

Three halves	Three minims		
Three quarters	Three crotchets		
Three eighths	Three quavers		
Three sixteenths	Three semiquavers		
Three thirty-seconds	Three demisemiquavers		
Three sixty-fourths	Three hemidemisemiquavers		

The whole-rest symbol is used to show exact time values in certain measures of long duration but it is also used as a sign to indicate a full measure of rest for any metric signature regardless of unit value. The whole-rest symbol, where used to show a full measure of rest, is placed directly under and attached to the fourth staff line and always in the middle of the measure. These placement conditions prevail where only one voice or part is on a staff.

Exceptions to this method of placing of the whole-rest occur (a) where two voices share a staff or (b) where cue notes are written into a part or score. In such instances the rest symbol must be placed below a line other than the fourth.

(a)   (b)

The half-rest symbol is placed directly on the third line in various horizontal positions in the measure, depending on which beat or beats it represents.

As with the whole-rest, a shared staff or cue notes necessitates a different line placement.

Where whole- or half-rests are used above or below a staff they must be used in conjunction with leger lines.

Rests of other values are placed in measures as needed according to the prevailing rhythm and meter, but not necessarily in the vertical center of the staff. Normally, however, (a) for a single part on a staff, or (b) for parts that share the same stems, they are centered vertically. A single rest will also suffice for two voices or parts having separate stems if the rhythm is obvious (c).

(a)   (b)   (c)

Sometimes independent voice motion makes it necessary to place a rest off-center, either in the upper or lower part of the staff.

Time dots are not used in conjunction with rests in simple meters.

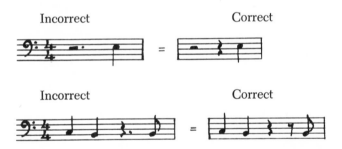

In compound meters, however, the dot is correct and easier to read than a corresponding rest.

Except for the whole-measure rest, rests must show the unit structure and measure values. A single longer rest may be used in place of two or more of lesser value only if the unit structure remains clear. In this respect, especial caution is advised in compound meters.

Incorrect

Correct

Rests encompassing more than one measure are indicated by a heavy horizontal line closed at each end and with a large numeral placed above the line, representing the number of silent measures.

Syncopation. There are no unusual problems concerning the notation of syncopation. As with notation of regular divisions, there should be absolute certainty regarding the unit of measure.

Substitution of longer note values for several notes of shorter duration is desirable.

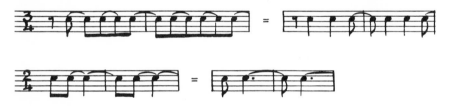

Long beams sometimes make reading easier.

The unit should always be discernible.

Incorrect   Correct

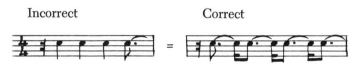

Abbreviations and Repeat Signs. Repetition of notes is often shown in abbreviated form by means of lines drawn through stems or placed under whole note heads, the number of lines indicating the note values and number of repetitions. Sometimes the first beat of a measure is fully notated to show the exact number of repetitions intended.

A definite number of repetitions per beat is called a *measured tremolo*. An indefinite number of note repetitions is called an *unmeasured tremolo* and is indicated by drawing at least three lines through the note stems. In order to avoid confusion with measured repeated thirty-second-notes, the term "tremolo," abbreviated "trem.," is often placed at the beginning of the tremolo passage.

Occasionally where thirty-second-note measured repetitions are called for, a figure "8" is placed above the first note with repeat lines to avoid confusion with unmeasured tremolo.

Another kind of abbreviated, repeated-note notation similar in purpose to that for single-note repetitions, also called tremolo, is that for alternating-note (trill-type) figures.

Where there is a definite number of alternations per beat, the figure is known as a *measured finger tremolo;* where the alternations are indefinite in number, the figure is known as *unmeasured finger tremolo*.

Note values for measured tremolos are shown by the number of beams between the alternating pitches, each written note of the figure being given the value that a single nonalternating note would have in the same relative position.

A newer method for notating the half-note values only, extends the beams to touch the note stems or combines long and short beams as in the last tremolo example below. There does not seem to be any particular merit in this, whereas the old system has the virtue of consistency in doubling the note values for any unit or combination of units.

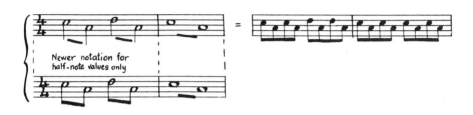

An unmeasured tremolo is indicated with three beams. In order to distinguish between that and a measured figure of thirty-second-notes it is best to place the term "tremolo" or its abbreviation "trem." above the staff at the beginning of the passage.

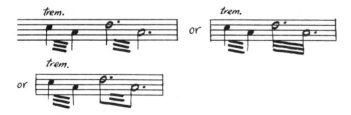

A repeat sign used primarily for instrumental parts and scores is the sign used to show repetition of the preceding measure only. It is particularly useful for measures of ostinato figures or chords. Observe that the repeated measures are numbered, the fully notated measure of the group being, of course, measure one.

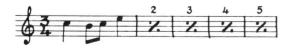

Repetition of two measures may be indicated by a similar sign.

Repeats within a measure are used to show repetition of continuously reiterated figures or chords in the same manner as that shown above for a full measure. The number of diagonal lines used in the figure is equal to the number of beams used in the regularly notated figure.

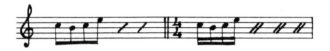

Chords repeated within a measure are sometimes indicated by stems without note heads. This notation is used mainly for popular music or as a type of shorthand for first drafts.

The octave sign may be considered to be an abbreviation since it does away with the need for numerous leger lines. Notes to be played an octave higher than written are given the sign 8 or *8va* placed directly above the first note of the passage and followed by a broken line extending over the duration of the passage. A short vertical line at the end of the passage marks the termination of the transposition. In most instances no other mark of cancellation is needed, though the addition of the term *loco* may serve as a safeguard.

Notes to be transposed by two octaves are marked as above but with *15* or *15ma* substituted for 8 or 8va. Two-octave transpositions are very rarely used.

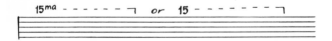

The same signs are used for transpositions one or two octaves lower by placing them below the staff.

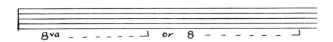

Octave transposition signs are used most often in keyboard music, reduced scores, and, occasionally, in full scores where space is limited. They should be avoided in instrumental parts, except where space is at a premium.

The signs indicating repetition of a section of a work are made with two bar lines in close proximity along with two dots placed in the two centered spaces of the staff. The dots are placed directly after or before the thin bar line.

If the repeat is to be made from the beginning of a work the first repeat sign is not necessary.

Repeat marks for two adjoining repeated sections are made with two heavy bars.

Occasionally a section of a work is repeated exactly except for a small portion at the end. In order to show the repetition of the section and later the changed portion at the end, first and second endings are indicated by the use of brackets and a repeat sign.

Da Capo, abbreviated D. C., means "from the head" or "from the beginning" and is used for the repetition of larger sections of a work. The sign is usually placed below the staff and indicates that the performer is to go back to the beginning of the piece and repeat an entire section.

D.C.

It is often used with the term "fine" (end, close), placed beneath the staff at the end of a work or at the end of a section of a work, to mark the termination of the Da Capo.

Dal Segno, abbreviated D. S., means "from the sign," and is a similar direction. It means to go back to and play from a point marked by the sign '$. , which is placed above the staff.

D.S.

Sometimes a D. C. or D. S. is used with the direction "al segno," meaning to go back either to the beginning or to the sign given above and to proceed as far as this new sign ⊕ , going from that point to a coda. This sign, like the other, is placed above the staff.

D.C. al ⊕

Accidentals. The term *accidental* is applied to sharps, flats, and multiples thereof indicating momentary changes for single notes or for all notes of like pitch occurring within a measure. The raising of a pitch by two semitones is indicated by this double-sharp sign x placed before the note. Lowering a pitch by two semitones is indicated by placing two flats before the note.

If notes of the same letter name but in different octaves are to be changed within the same measure, it is necessary to use an accidental before the first note changed in each octave.

Any sign of chromatic alteration is in effect throughout the balance of the measure in which it appears, except in certain contemporary works, in which accidentals apply only to the note immediately affected by the sign. In such cases an explanatory note is usually made at the beginning of the work.

With the exception of the case noted above, any accidental, in theory, is cancelled in the following measure. In practice, however, it is safer to add a natural sign when the change occurs at the beginning of the measure.

Altered pitches that are tied over a bar line remain altered in the new measure. An accidental must be placed in front of the next note of the same pitch as the tied note if it is also to be altered.

Any change from a multiple sharp or flat to a single sharp or flat or natural requires only the single new accidental; the old practice of using compound accidentals to show cancellation or change is no longer observed.

Old notation   New notation

Two parts or voices on one staff that are played by a single player require writing of accidentals only once regardless of crossing of the parts. Where the staff is shared by parts for two different players, however, it is best to repeat the accidentals as needed in each voice.

Where two voices or parts on the same staff have different note values played simultaneously, all accidentals must be placed on the same side of the note heads. Observe that the accidentals for the notes of the octave are in a vertical line.

Incorrect   Correct

In the following example the notes A and G♯ on the third beat are not in the customary ascending order; this misplacement is done in order to have the note of longer value ahead of the short note.

Vertical placement of multiple signs is made according to the position of ascending pitches wherever possible, but the reverse order of the accidentals is sometimes needed in order to keep a compact visual pattern within the staff.

Notes with the same letter names but with differing accidentals played simultaneously are found frequently in contemporary music. If one of the notes is natural it is necessary to use the natural sign if the differing pitches are written on the same staff.

Arpeggios. Arpeggio signs are placed directly in front of the chords to be broken. The chords are normally sounded from the low note to the high note. If a reversed arpeggio is intended, the chord to be broken from top note to bottom note, the regular arpeggio sign must either have an arrow pointing the direction preceding it or have an arrow head attached to its lower extremity. These arrows must also be used where arpeggios alternate the direction of roll.

For arpeggio notation applying specifically to two-staff instruments refer to Chapter 4, page 60.

Clef Changes. When a clef changes during the progress of a work, the new sign is written immediately before the first note affected by the change.

If the clef change takes place at the beginning of a measure, the new clef sign is placed before the bar line marking the beginning of that measure. This is done even if the clef change occurs on a new line or on a new page.

Where a clef change is preceded by rests, the new clef sign is placed directly before the notes of change if the first note is on the beginning of a beat.

If the notes of change begin on a fractional beat, the new clef is placed directly in front of the rest marking the silent portion of the beat.

Key and Meter Changes. Changes of key and meter signature are traditionally marked with a double bar wherever such a change occurs.

Today, however, this practice is not observed for changes of meter, the changes being placed after a single bar line. The same procedure is sometimes followed for changes of key signature, although the double bar is still widely used. Another new idea now commonly used is the omission of cancellation signs (naturals), going directly into the new key without them.

Old

New

A change of key seems to stand out with greater clarity when a double bar is used. The foregoing example is better with a combination of old and new practices.

Combined

Any metric change involving a change of basic unit should show the intended relative tempo of the new unit by use of note symbols placed above the staff as shown below.

A change from any key requiring a signature to either C major or A minor must show cancellation of the accidentals regardless of the bar line system used, for obvious reasons.

Changes of clef, key signature, or meter signature that take place at the beginning of a new line should be anticipated by indicating the change on the old line in addition to placing the new signature(s) on the new line. Where all three are to be changed, the clef change is made only on the new line.

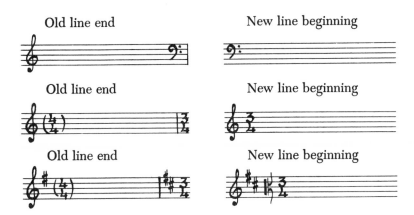

Performance Directions. Placement of the various symbols and verbal directions for giving performance information is quite consistent. Some of these are normally placed above the staff, some below the staff and others both above and below the staff.

Tempo indications, such as Allegro, Adagio, Slowly, and so forth, are placed above the staff in all scores and parts.

Metronome marks are used to supplement verbal directions indicating tempo at the beginning of a work, or they may be used alone. The marks are used with or without parentheses, but the use of parentheses would seem to be superfluous. Metronome marks are also used during the course of a work to clarify changes in tempo and/or meter.

Ornament signs such as those for a mordent  or for a turn also go above the staff. Today, such ornamental figures are written out in full notation except where there can be no doubt as to the intention of the sign.

Dynamic signs are placed below the staff wherever possible. In music for instruments requiring two staves they are placed between the staves. In vocal music they are placed above the staves. The signs should be carefully placed, exactly below or above the first note of the passage affected. Directions for crescendo and diminuendo, whether verbal or by the signs ⌐ ¬ should show an exact terminal volume level.

Heavy accent directions, such as sforzando and sforzato, are usually abbreviated (*sf* and *sfz*) and are placed below the staff in instrumental music or between the staves of keyboard music. The same is true of the forte-piano sign, *fp*.

Marcato signs, ∧ and ∨, are placed above or below note heads, opposite the direction of the stems. The sign always points away from the note head.

Accents, >; *tenuto marks,* —; and *staccato marks,* ᛧ , ᛧ are placed next to note heads wherever possible.

Where there are note clusters or chords with seconds the marks are placed over the "correct" side of the note stem.

The *fermata*, or hold, is usually placed above the staff. When placed below the staff, as for the lower voice on a shared staff, the sign is used in reversed position.

Exceptions to the placement of performance directions as shown above and additional signs and directions for specific instrumental notation are discussed in Chapter 4.

Glissandos are shown either by a straight line or by a wavy line drawn between the terminal note heads with the abbreviation "*gliss.*" placed over the line. Where two or more notes on the same staff progress simultaneously as glissandos, lines must be drawn between the two notes of each voice or part. Today, however, the lines are often used without the term.

Trills. A trill on a single note is indicated by the sign *tr* placed above the note. Longer trills extending over several tied notes must have the trill sign over the first note and a wavy line extending over the remaining tied notes. Where the trilled note continues on to a new score line, the wavy line must also be extended.

The trilling note is always the pitch of the note immediately above the main note as determined by the diatonic scale. Any chromatic deviation from this is indicated by placing an accidental next to or above the trill sign. Sometimes a small, stemless note head placed in parentheses is used.

Auxiliary notes at the end of a trill are written with small note heads and beams and with stems extending upward. Two or three notes are written with sixteenth-note values and four notes with thirty-second-note values.

If the trill is to begin with the auxiliary note, the small note is written in front of the main note.

Double trills must have an additional trill sign beneath the lower note.

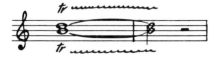

Slurs. Slurs are used to show legato in all types of music. In string music they serve the additional function of indicating bowing procedure.

The placement of slurs is determined mainly by the stemming of the notes affected by the slur. In general, slurs are placed at the heads of notes. When note stems extend in both directions, slurs are placed above the staff regardless of the division of stem direction.

Slurs always start and end either over or under the center of a note head. Where the beginning or the end of the slur is over a note stem, the stem itself serves as the mark for the terminal point. Ties are an exception to this rule.

Other exceptions to this practice will sometimes occur in scores with closely-spaced staves, keyboard music, shared staves or in bowings. These are discussed in Chapter 4.

Slurs connecting two or more notes of equal pitch are called *ties* and are always placed to connect note heads. Where more than two notes are tied, the slurs must extend from note head to note head of the notes of the tied group; a single slur for more than two notes of equal pitch cannot serve as an indication for a tie.

Incorrect   Correct

The slurs for a single voice tie always curve in the direction opposite that of the note stems.

Where ties and legato slurs are combined each should observe its own respective placement procedures. The curve directions will sometimes coincide and will sometimes be opposed.

A single slur is sufficient to show legato for a progression of chords.

Where there are several tied notes on one stem, the ties curve in opposite directions for the outside notes; the curve directions for the ties of the other notes are determined by their position on the staff, relative to the middle staff line, wherever possible.

Where the notes are all either high or low on the staff, the ties are balanced.

Where chords contain a second, ties on the notes of that interval must curve in opposite directions no matter what the staff position may be; this may cause a majority of the ties to curve in one direction.

Ties and slurs for legato chord progressions curve in opposite directions if there is only one tied pitch; with more than one tied pitch the slurs for the ties will curve in both directions. The latter method of notation is clearer.

Occasionally   Preferred

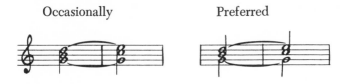

Ties and legato slurs combined within a single measure should be avoided by reducing the tied notes to a single note if possible.

Not this   This

Where a succession of legato chords contains notes of like pitch, the legato slur must be placed at a point where it will not be mistaken for a tie.

Where performance signs, such as staccato dots, tenuto lines, and others, are combined with slurs, they are normally placed between the slur and the note head.

Accents used with ties are placed outside the slur.

Accents used with legato slurs will vary in their placement according to the available room, the compactness of the total assembly, and the arc of the slurs. In the illustration below, the first example (a) balances because of a sign over each note head; the second example (b) shows the accent outside the slur in order to keep a more horizontal position of the slurs; the third example (c) shows two different accent placements in order to give the best positions for the slurs.

(a)   (b)   (c)

Many of the procedures discussed in this section on performance directions must be disregarded when two voices share a staff and have independent motion. Deviations occur often in ensemble scores and in keyboard music. Examples of notation for specific circumstances are shown in Chapter 4.

Rehearsal (Location) Signs. Rehearsal numbers and letters, sometimes called location numbers and letters, are identification points in scores and parts meant to facilitate rehearsal by permitting quick common reference to a given section of the work being rehearsed.

Where numbers are used, measures are usually counted in groups of ten, starting with the first full measure. At the beginning of the tenth measure, the number ten, enclosed in a box (10), is placed above the staff. Beginning with the eleventh measure, ten more measures are counted off to point twenty (20). This procedure is continued to the end of the piece. Where there are several movements in a work the numbering begins again with each movement.

The use of rehearsal letters is usually reserved for the division of the piece or movement into longer sections of unequal measure count. The letters are placed at strategic places: change of key, change of mood, change of texture, or the beginning of a passage having excessive technical demands. The indications are in alphabetical order, and the letters are boxed in the same manner as rehearsal numbers:

The preference today seems to be for numbers, although both methods are used. A good case can be made for the use of either. The equal-measure division affords an easy means for checking parts and for copying and proofreading; on the other hand, letters placed with unequal measure grouping are usually better located in regard to musical sections or rehearsal demands. In either case, the location sign must be placed exactly at the beginning of a measure without any overlapping of the preceding one.

Four less common methods of marking location points with numbers should be mentioned. In the first, numbers are placed at prospective rehearsal points in the same manner as rehearsal letters, the first point being marked 1 , the next 2 , continuing through as many numbers as necessary.

The second method makes use of true measure numbers, the measure selected being a desired rehearsal point. For example, the first point might be at measure sixteen $\boxed{16}$, the next at measure thirty-five $\boxed{35}$, and so forth, continuing as needed for rehearsal purposes.

The third method uses numbers in numerical order to mark equal-measure sections.

Rehearsal numbers or letters are extremely important to insure efficient use of rehearsal time for any music involving more than one performer. Whatever system is used should be retained throughout a given work.

PRAIRIE SCHOONER by Anthony Donato: Copyright 1957 by The Composers Press, Inc.
Used by permission.

SPECIAL NOTATION FOR SPECIFIC AREAS

T HE NOTATION PRACTICES of Chapter 3 apply to all music. The additional symbols and notation procedures of this chapter apply either chiefly or exclusively to limited instrumental and vocal areas.

KEYBOARD INSTRUMENTS AND HARP

Many of the deviations in notation for this group of instruments are due to the fact that their music is notated on a double-staff score line. Although music for organ has a third staff for the pedals, the notation for the manuals is the same as that for the other keyboard instruments.

Arpeggios. Where independent arpeggio signs are placed in front of simultaneously played chords on each staff, it means that each hand will begin its chord roll at the same time.

Where the arpeggio sign runs unbroken through both staves, it signifies a continuous arpeggio starting with the low note.

Arpeggiated chords always progress from the low note to the high note; arpeggiating simultaneously in the opposite direction, continuously in the opposite direction, or with the hands rolling in opposite directions, or alternating directions of roll with any of these combinations requires the use of arrows to show direction as explained in Chapter 3, pages 46-47.

No arpeggio sign should be used in harp music unless a decided roll is desired, since there is a normal tendency to roll all chords.

If simultaneous, non-arpeggiated sounding of chords for the harp is to be assured, a bracket should be placed in front of the chords. The terms *dry* or *sec* are also used for this purpose.

Beams Between Staves. It is sometimes necessary or desirable to beam notes on both staves together in order to improve the readability of a figure or to emphasize a musical line. Under most conditions, left-hand notes are placed on the lower staff and right-hand notes on the upper. Excessive use of leger lines should be avoided by changing the clef sign for the hand in question. Occasionally, where there are long, continuous figures or arpeggios, the staff-hand distinction is not observed, the hand choice being left to the discretion of the performer.

Beamed figures between the staves are often used to replace flags and rests in order to give a cleaner look to the score for easier reading.

Extra Staves. In piano music, an extra staff is sometimes needed to allow for independent motion for a voice or to avoid crowding of the notes on the two regular staves. The additional staff may be used for treble or bass clef as needed.

Glissandos. For keyboard instruments, notation of glissandos is the same as that for most other instruments as shown in Chapter 3, page 51.

Glissandos for harp are possible only on chords or scales having from four to seven different pitches. Pedal settings or enharmonic unisons must be accurately indicated.

The following examples show three different methods for notating the chord F♯-A-C-E♭.

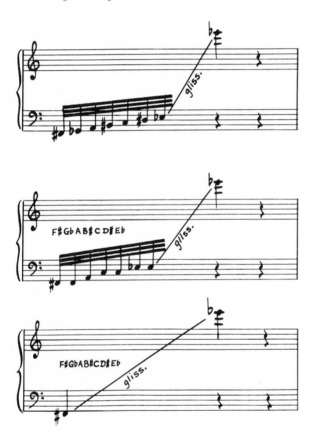

Harmonics. Harmonics for the harp are indicated by a small circle placed over the notes. It is possible to play two notes at once with the left hand, but only one with the right hand. There are two methods of notation. The first method, corresponding to the notation of the octave harmonic in string music, shows the actual pitch of the note with a circle over it to indicate a harmonic. The second method, which seems to be the one most often used, shows the note with a circle over it, one octave *below* the actual sounding pitch. It is advisable to include an explanatory note referring to the system used in the harp part.

The two notation systems are shown below.

Sounds as written   Sounds

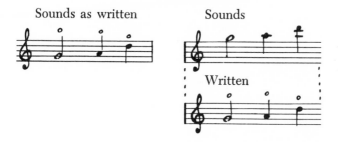

Written

Pedal Marks. In much piano music pedaling is left to the discretion of the performer, and no pedal signs are given. When signs are used they refer most often to the damper pedal. They are placed beneath the lower staff and show points for both depressing and releasing the pedal. There are several methods of showing the use of the damper pedal, the one most often used probably being the abbreviation *Ped.* to indicate depressing the pedal and an asterisk * placed at the end of the pedaled passage to show the release.

Use of brackets for pedal signs is more modern.

Brackets showing continuous pedaling have two versions.

The term *una corda,* abbreviated U. C., is used to mark the use of the left (soft) pedal and is placed beneath the lower staff of a score. It is cancelled by use of the term *tre corde,* abbreviated T. C., also placed beneath the lower staff.

The middle, or sustaining, pedal is less often called for; if a direction is needed, the abreviation Sust. Ped. or S. P. placed below the beginning of the passage is used with a bracket extending the length of the passage affected. If damper-pedal marks are also needed, they are placed below those for the sustaining pedal.

Pedals on the harp are used only for changing the pitches of the strings. The pitch settings are shown in three ways. In the first, all seven scale degrees are given in succession with their desired accidentals.

The second way is similar to the first, but the pedal letters are arranged according to left- and right-foot groupings, the right-foot grouping being placed above the left-foot grouping.

The third way makes use of a diagram showing relative pedal positions. Marks above the horizontal line represent pedals in the flat position, those on the line representing the natural position and those below the line, the sharp position.

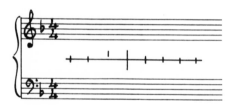

Subsequent pedal changes need to show only the changed pitch, when letters are used, or a revised version of the diagram. There is no uniformity of opinion regarding the best point at which to show a pedal change. Some harpists prefer it in advance of the change, whereas others like to have the symbol change directly above the place affected.

Pedal indications for organ are sometimes made to show which foot is to be used and whether it is to be toe or heel. The symbol for toe is ∧ and that for heel is ∩ . Placed above the staff, the signs apply to the right foot and below the staff to the left foot.

These signs are rarely used by composers; they are used mainly for study purposes.

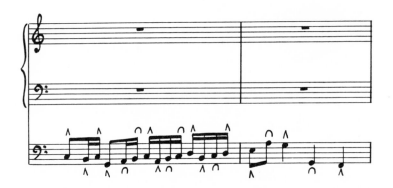

Registration. Organ registration directions are placed at the beginning of a composition at the left side of the first page, above the tempo indication. In some editions they are placed in the left page margin at the sides of the staves. Directions are usually of a general nature, since organs vary in their capacities and may or may not be capable of being set for an unusual registration. In listing registrations the manual stops are given first.

During the course of the composition, changes are shown as they occur, either above the manual staff affected or above the pedal staff.

Repeat Signs. With the exception of signs for single note, chord, or alternating note repetitions, repeat signs for single measure repetition are not used much in keyboard music notation. They are best reserved for preliminary sketches of works and should not appear in final copies. For this purpose, the symbol indicating repetition of an entire measure can be useful for ostinato figures. Where the notes of the figure are beamed between staves the repeat symbol is placed as shown below. Note that each repeated measure is numbered, the fully-notated measure being number one.

Slurs. The use of slurs in music for keyboard instruments and harp follows the procedures discussed in Chapter 3, wherever possible. Deviations, however, will occur fairly frequently, depending on the proximity of the notes between the staves and the number of dynamics and other performance directions.

The rule for placing slurs over note heads holds good for similar motion in the two hands if the beams and performance directions do not take up too much space.

In many cases where each hand covers a considerable range and there are dynamic indications between the staves, slurs are best placed above the treble staff and below the bass staff in order to avoid crowding.

Where legato slurs, ties, and dynamic marks are combined, many of the slurs may be on the "wrong" side.

Slurs enclosing small groups of notes having staccato dots or tenuto lines to indicate portato are placed over or under note heads, wherever possible, not over or under the stems and beams.

Staff Selection. Under most conditions each staff represents notes to be played by one hand. Occasionally, however, parts for both hands are written on one staff. The choice of placing notes for both hands on one staff or for changing a clef sign in order to keep separate staves must be determined by the clarity of the result. Ease of reading is the prime consideration; crowding of notes and excessive use of leger lines are to be avoided.

In the first section of the following example, notice that no rests are written for the top staff in the first measure or for the lower staff in the third measure.

Moderato

This is an alternative way for notation of the same example.

Moderato

These two notations are virtually equal in ease of reading.

A third way of writing the same example is not good, owing to the excessive number of leger lines.

Moderato

Sympathetic Vibration (Piano). This effect is achieved on the piano by silently pressing down keys for desired sounds and holding them down while other notes are actually being played, the sound for the silently depressed keys being produced by sympathetic vibration of the open strings. The notation for this effect is the same as that used to indicate harmonics in notation for stringed instruments, that is, diamonded-shaped note heads.

Tone Clusters (Keyboard Instruments). Combinations of notes exceeding in number those playable by normal fingering or demanding unusual percussive power are sometimes played by fist, palm of hand, or forearm. The indication is made at the desired point by the abbreviations R. F. and L. F. for right and left fist and R. A. and L. A. for right and left arm, or the direction "palm of hand."

Henry Cowell, the originator of these effects, has devised a notation system which is quite simple. Clusters composed of all or many continuously chromatic notes are written with a double stem or a heavy stem between the extreme pitches.

Where only black keys are to be played for the cluster, a sharp is placed above the cluster symbol. Where only white keys are to be used, a natural sign is placed above the cluster symbol.

STRINGS

Alternating Unisons. The effect of alternating an open string with a string stopped to the same pitch is notated by alternate stem directions and a small circle over the open-string notes.

Bowings. Down bow and up bow signs need be used only at the beginning of a passage or where there is a succession of notes to be played in the same direction. The signs are placed above the staff.

In string music, notes within the limits of a slur are to be played in one bow. Each new bowing slur indicates a change of bow direction.

A slur within a slur shows both bowing and phrasing, the longer slur being the bowing sign. Bowing slurs, whenever possible, are placed over or under note heads, not over or under stems and beams.

Slurs are not used to mark phrases alone, although bowings and phrases may coincide. In the following example the outer slur is the bowing and the inner slurs mark articulation.

The bowing known as *louré* is written with tenuto lines in combination with a slur; it corresponds to the portato in piano music. In string music, the tenuto mark means a semi-legato note articulation much more often than a lengthening of time value.

Dots are used for both staccato and spiccato effects, the tempo and style of the music determining which interpretation is to be made. The dots are placed next to the note heads wherever possible.

The wedge symbol for a heavier staccato is also placed next to the note head.

Where dots are combined with a bowing slur, the intention may be for a group of solid staccato notes to be played in one bow, as shown in the first part of the example below; a springing arpeggio across the strings, as shown in the second part of the example, or a ricochet (*jeté*), as shown in the third part of the example.

Divisi. Division of a part is marked by placing the abbreviation "div." (divisi) above the staff at the desired point. The most common division is into two parts, the two players at each stand of a section making the same division. Where time values are the same, notes in divided parts may be written on one stem.

Where the time values of the notes differ, separate stems are necessary.

Division may be made in more than two parts, the indication then being *div. a 3* (or by 3), or 4, or whatever number is necessary.

Independent motion of the parts may require more than one staff. Multiple staves are connected with a bracket with the division indication placed in the side margin of the page in front of the bracket.

Occasionally division is to be made by stands rather than by players; for this, the indication *div. by stands* is used.

Where all players return to the same part, it is marked with the term *unisono*, or *unison*, abbreviated *unis*.

A division on one staff must show consistently the separate voices where there is alternating division and unison.

Harmonics. The sign for a natural harmonic is a small circle placed over the note at actual pitch. With the exception of the harmonic one octave above the pitch of the open string, all the others can be produced at more than one point on the same string. These alternate points are notated with diamond-shaped note heads. Shown below are the natural harmonics of the violin G string and the most useful (not all) of the alternate points; in each case, these sound the same pitch as the main note.

Artificial harmonics most often used are those formed by intervals of fourths and fifths, fourths being more common. In notating the first type, the lower note is written as a solid-headed note with a diamond-shaped note placed a perfect fourth above it. The actual sound is a pitch two octaves above the solid note. In notating the second type, the diamond-shaped note head is placed a perfect fifth above the solid note head, and the actual sound is a twelfth above the solid note.

The practice of simply writing circles over notes to be sounded as harmonics and leaving their method of production up to the player is not to be recommended.

High Notes. High notes in string parts should be written with leger lines at their actual pitch, not an octave lower with an octave sign. Players tend to read by relating note position on a staff with fingering. Leger lines should also be used in scores wherever possible, although the close proximity of staves, along with performance directions, often makes it necessary to resort to octave signs.

Miscellaneous Signs. The indications *col legno* (with the wood), *sul ponticello* (near the bridge), and *sul tasto* (over the fingerboard), are written above the staff. The direction for a return to normal tone is shown by the term *modo ordinario* or *normal*.

The special effect of striking the back of the instrument with a knuckle is notated with an "X" for a note head and the verbal direction, "strike back of instrument with knuckle."

Mutes. The use of a mute is indicated by the term *con sordino*, abbreviated "sord." (plural *sordini*), or *with mute*, placed above the staff. Removal of the mute is directed by the term *senza sordino*, or *mute off*. A few silent beats must be allowed for either affixing or removing the mute.

Pizzicato. The abbreviation *pizz.* is placed above the staff to indicate a passage to be plucked. Resumption of use of the bow is shown by the term *arco,* also placed above the staff.

The notes of pizzicato chords are usually played as simultaneously as possible; if they are to be arpeggiated, the arpeggio sign is used.

Double stops that are to be plucked simultaneously rather than arpeggiated are given a bracket in front of the notes.

Consecutive pizzicato chords in fast tempo are played by alternating the direction of striking the strings. The effect may be notated by use of up and down bow signs or by arrows, the first way being preferred.

Pizzicato is also combined with harmonics, sul ponticello, and sul tasto.

Pizzicato is sometimes used in combination with glissando for intervals not exceeding a fourth or fifth. The effect is best with a high level of sound.

The short slur, used to show continuing vibration, should be used only over notes of long duration, since it is illogical to call for continuing sound while specifying rests at the same time.

Not this   This

The very explosive kind of pizzicato played by pulling the string away from the fingerboard and letting it snap back is indicated by the sign ∮ .

Left-hand pizzicato is shown by a small cross placed above or below the plucked note.

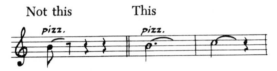

This effect may also be used in combination with arco.

String Indication. The designation of the string to be used is made by writing the desired Roman numeral above the staff, I always being used for the highest string. Another method is to write the name of the string above the staff.

Tremolos. Bowed and fingered tremolos are notated as described in Chapter 3, page 40. The fingered tremolos may be played with either single bow strokes (a) for each note, or (b) connected, the latter being far more common.

Either type of tremolo is often combined with sul ponticello; the bowed type is also used with harmonics.

WOODWINDS AND BRASS

The notation principles of Chapter 3 will serve, with a few exceptions, for nearly all woodwind and brass requirements.

Key Signatures. In much of today's music key signatures are omitted entirely, accidentals being written in front of notes as needed. This means that for transposing instruments there is no staff identification by means of a key signature to show what the transposition may be, which makes it extremely important to have the transpositions of the instrument listed in the score in front of the staff lines concerned.

In orchestra scores it is customary not to use key signatures for horns, except in educational music, even though all the other instruments may have them. In some scores the practice of eliminating signatures is extended to all transposing instruments. Modern usage tends toward elimination of key signatures for all instruments.

The same remarks apply to band scores, except that signatures are sometimes used for the horns when other instruments have them, particularly in educational music.

High Notes. High notes in wind parts should always be written at the actual pitch with leger lines, not an octave lower with an octave sign. Leger lines should also be used in scores unless space is very limited.

Legatos. Slurs in woodwind and brass music show legato passages to be played smoothly and may or may not coincide with phrase and breath points. Whether they are over notes of varying pitches or notes of like pitches, slurs mark the smoothest manner of execution.

Slurs in combination with dots or tenuto lines indicate a lesser degree of smoothness.

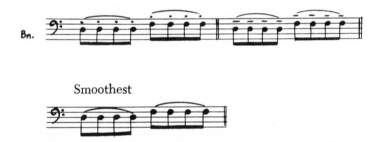

Mutes. The indication for the use of a mute in woodwind and brass music is the same as that used for strings, *con sordino* (sord.) or *with mute,* placed above the staff. A return to normal tone is shown by *senza sordino* or *open,* the latter sometimes shown by the sign O. Unless a special type of mute is called for in the score, the player will use a regular mute. On the horn, muting may also be done with the hand.

Fully stopped notes on the horn are indicated by placing crosses above each note, by use of the term *stopped,* or both. The harsh effect produced by overblown stopped notes is shown by marking the notes with crosses and adding the term *brassy* or its French equivalent, *cuivré.*

Sharing a Staff. When two parts share the same staff in a score they may use the same note stems for different pitches if time values are equal. For different time values, the stems must point in opposite directions. When both parts are to play the same notes, the indication a2 must be placed above the staff or stems must point in both directions. If the unison passage is short and there is a return to independent notes, the double stems are preferred.

If one part drops out, rests must accurately indicate this, and the continuing part is marked to avoid error. After the measure with rests, stems for the continuing part follow "correct" stemming procedures unless the other part is to resume in a short time, in which case the single direction stems and the rests are continued.

Separate parts with equal time values may share stems only when there are no unison pitches.

Possible   Correct

At the beginning of a work or after a long rest, if only one part is to play, it is sufficient to place a number 1 or 2 above or below the staff to mark the entry; rests are not necessary for the silent part.

If both instruments are to play from the beginning of a work or passage it is essential to write the term a2 above the staff.

If the unison passage continues after a page turn in a score, the term should be placed in parenthesis on the appropriate line of the new page.

Dynamics and other performance directions are written beneath the staff, one set of indications serving for two instruments sharing a staff unless the parts move independendently; in such an instance, two sets of directions, one above and one below the staff, will be necessary.

Tonguing. All single notes in woodwind and brass music are articulated by tonguing, the degree of separation being determined by the performance marking, the speed, and the character of the music. Double and triple tonguing need not be marked in a score or part, but if they are needed in educational music, they are shown as in the following example.

The special effect known as *flutter tongue* is signified by placing the term itself above the staff, by drawing three lines through note stems, or by combined use of both. Another method is the use of the term *flutter*, followed by a wavy line over the passage.

PERCUSSION

The principles of Chapter 3 apply to all percussion instruments with regard to rhythm and to instruments of definite pitch for many of the pitch notations.

Clef Signs for Indefinite Pitch Instruments. Papers especially ruled for orchestra or band instrumentation include several single lines for notating percussion parts. Where ordinary staff paper is used, the identification of the staves used for percussion instruments of indefinite pitch is done in several ways. Some notation practice gives the treble clef sign to the instruments with higher, lighter timbres and the bass clef to the "heavier" instruments. Another version reserves the treble clef for melodic instruments and gives the bass clef to all instruments of indefinite pitch.

Today one often finds a plain staff without a clef sign used for instruments of indefinite pitch. Sometimes a neutral sign, written ⊞════, is used to indicate instruments of indefinite pitch. Either of the last two systems seems preferable to the first two.

Key Signatures. In traditional notation, key signatures are used for some of the percussion instruments of definite pitch. These instruments are the xylophone, the marimba, the glockenspiel, and the vibraphone. Present practice tends to use accidentals as needed, rather than key signatures. Timpani are never given a key signature.

Miscellaneous Directions. It should be assumed that single notes and repeated notes are intended to sound as notated. Flams, drags, and similar figures should be written accurately into a score.

Frequently instruments of indefinite pitch of the same kind are used in multiples to give a "high-low" effect by utilizing different sizes. Wood blocks, bongo drums, and others are often used in this manner. In notating such effects, lines or spaces on a staff are used simply to show approximate relative pitch spacings.

Bongos

In the case of temple blocks, which, in sets of five, approximate the intervals of a pentatonic scale, the relative pitches may be indicated by a pentatonic note sequence on the staff.

Temple blocks

A symbol depicting a triangle and beater ◿ is sometimes used to indicate use of the triangle.

Glissando effects on timpani are written to show termination points.

Special directions for sticks to be used on timpani, suspended cymbal, tambourine, bass drum, and other instruments are written above the percussion line or staff. Dynamic marks and similar directions go below the staff or line, unless two instruments sharing a staff require separate directions.

The short slur used to indicate continuing reverberation on a note in a part for cymbals, triangle, gong or any other reverberating instrument should be used only on notes of long duration. It is illogical to call for continuing sound and then place a rest immediately after such a sign.

Incorrect   Correct

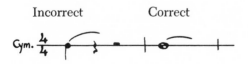

The opposite incongruity is the use of such terms as *sec, dry,* and *choke.* If rests in percussion parts are observed for their true values as in other instrumental parts, notes of short values with staccato dots are sufficient to show any desired degree of cut-off sound. Why should it be necessary to supplement an eighth-note with a dot over it, followed by rests, with the additional direction, *choke?*

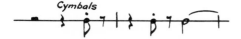

Diamond-shaped note heads (◇) are sometimes written in cymbal parts. "X" symbols for notes of short duration are often used in parts for cymbals and other instruments of indefinite pitch.

Rolls, Tremolos, Trills. These terms may be considered to be synonymous when used for most percussion instruments. The fact that chimes, glockenspiel, marimba, timpani, vibraphone, and xylophone can, at least in theory, produce a true trill on two closely adjacent pitches, whereas instruments of indefinite pitch cannot, serves only to point out another of the inaccuracies of music notation.

In general, rolls notated as trills or tremolos seem to be used about equally for instruments of indefinite pitch and for timpani. Since timpani pitches must be pre-set there is no danger of mistaking the intent of a trill sign. For some of the other instruments of definite pitch, however, true trills are not only possible but also frequently used; notational distinction, therefore, should be carefully observed by using the tremolo sign for repeated-note rolls.

Rolls should be written with or without ties to show accurately whether they are continuous or broken. Termination points should also be clear.

In the following example, sections (a) and (b) show two methods for notating a continuous roll with termination points. Sections (c) and (d) show a series of broken rolls with termination points.

Measured tremolos are not used as frequently for percussion instruments as they are for other instruments. If they are used, the first unit value should be written out in full notation.

Rolls for the tambourine are sometimes differentiated by specifying the tremolo sign for a shake and the trill sign for a thumb roll. The words *shake* or *thumb roll* are added.

Alternating-note figure tremolos for instruments of definite pitch are unmeasured far more often than they are measured. If a measured tremolo is to be used, the first unit value of the passage should be written out in full-value notation in order to avoid any error of interpretation.

Staff Placement. As we mentioned earlier, score papers ruled especially for orchestra or band scoring have several single lines on which to notate the parts for instruments of indefinite pitch. On regular staff paper, any needed number of staves may be given to the notation of percussion parts. For simultaneous playing, not more than two parts should be written on any one staff. This does not mean instruments; there is no reasonable limit to the number of different instruments that may be notated on one staff or to be played by one player, as long as there is sufficient time for the player to change instruments. In any case, the important thing is to place the notation for any given instrument on the same staff degree throughout a given composition. At the point of entry of each new instrument, the name of the entering instrument should be written above the staff. As a further precaution the note stems for a given instrument should always point in the same direction.

The next example shows a percussion part written on two staves, requiring four players in addition to the timpanist.

VOCAL MUSIC

The chief difference between the traditional notation of vocal music and that of instrumental music is the beaming and flagging of notes. There is some movement today toward coordination of vocal and instrumental notation, and some publishers are issuing vocal music in the instrumental manner, but the practice is not yet extensive.

Beams and Flags. Traditionally, notes of less than quarter-note value receive separate flags for each word of text. Any extension of the word through more than one pitch is shown by beaming the notes. Syllables are treated in the same manner. Beams, when so used, are often at wide variance with unit beaming, as seen in instrumental notation, and have nothing to do with the regularity of unit division.

Performance Directions. Dynamic signs and any special performance directions are placed above the staff in vocal music in order not to interfere with the text.

When __ they re - turn to him.

Slurs. Slurs are used in vocal music to mark legato extensions on words or syllables. Where beamed notes used in the traditional manner show such legato extension, the slurs are still used and are supplementary. In most cases, as in the example below, the beam in the third measure would not be sufficient by itself, since it does not include all of the eighth notes of the legato passage.

re - joice _____ in our hab - i - ta - tion

Texts. Words for any vocal music should be used just as they appear in the original source if the text is used intact. This means that any punctuation marks, capitalizations, and any other features of the text must be used without exception, regardless of the distortion of sentence structure caused by musical means. Any free adaptation of an original text should be so indicated.

Syllabic division of words is made in the accepted standard fashion found in any good dictionary. Divisions are hyphenated; when the division extends over the duration of several notes, the syllables are separated by widely-spaced hyphens.

The extension of words through the duration of several tied notes or notes of varying pitch is shown by a solid line extending along the type line. Any punctuation marks in the text at that point must precede the line.

all. Let___ ev - ery thing go, ____

If the text is to be lettered by hand, it is best to rule guide lines in order to make the letters uniform in size.

When a text is typed on transparent paper, a sheet of carbon paper should be placed in reverse on the back of the sheet so that the letters will be sufficiently black for good reproduction.

Narration and Spoken Song. Vocal parts that are not intended to be sung may be (1) free speaking parts written without regard for either rhythm or pitch; (2) parts spoken to specified rhythmic values, but without pitch; and (3) parts that are written with both specific rhythms and implied pitches. The third type is commonly called *sprechstimme*. This German term, however, may be applied more accurately to any spoken part.

Vocal parts to be spoken freely, without regard for rhythm or pitch, are written in the normal score position under a blank, but metered, staff; the words are spread to cover the approximate time span, determined by the tempo of the music, needed for speaking them (a). At times, where it may be necessary to set a fairly long portion of the text to a note grouping of short duration, the words must be grouped above the musical material (b). This same procedure is used when the text is spoken to held chords (c).

(a)   (b)

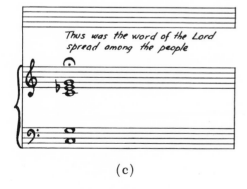

(c)

Narrative parts spoken to specified rhythms, but without pitch, can be notated in three ways: (a) The text is written below a single line on which

the rhythm is indicated by standard note symbols; (b) The rhythm is indicated on an arbitrary line or space of a metered staff without a clef sign,
by standard note symbols; (c) The rhythm is indicated by headless note-
stems extending down from the third space of a metered staff without a
clef sign. The third method has the disadvantage of not being able to
show open-head note values and is best suited to narration in fast tempos
with rhythmic patterns of short duration.

In all three methods any change of inflection is determined by the music
and/or text and is left to the discretion of the speaker.

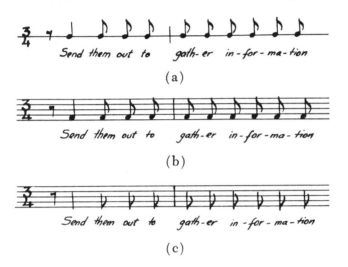

Vocal parts written to specific rhythmic values and pitches, introduced
by Schoenberg in *Pierrot Lunaire,* are meant to combine speech and song.
The notation of this type of vocal part is intended to show inflection and
tessitura, though the degree of pitch is not exact. Standard note symbols
are used, but the stems of all notes to be spoken are marked with a cross.

A second method for notating the same spoken-song effect, first used
by Schoenberg in *Ode to Napoleon,* employs standard note symbols placed
on or near a single line. The placement of the symbols shows the relative
rise or fall of the pitch.

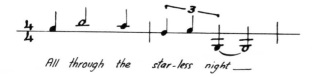

All through the   star-less night ___

From the standpoint of notation, it would seem that the first method is better able to indicate tessitura. In actual performance, however, the results are usually quite similar.

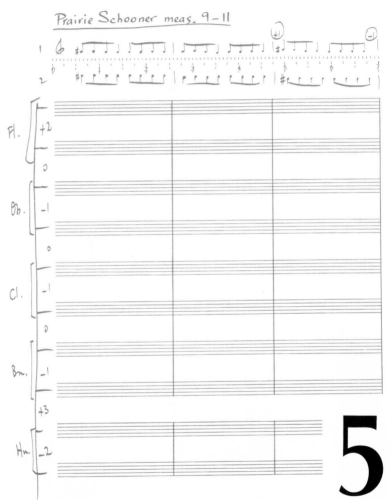

PRAIRIE SCHOONER by Anthony Donato: Copyright 1957 by The Composers Press, Inc. Used by permission.

5

SPACING AND ALIGNMENT

CHAPTERS 3 AND 4 deal with the basic materials of music notation with regard to their proper formation and staff placement, chiefly as individual symbols. The placing of this basic material on a page of blank music paper in a manner resulting in neatness, clarity of purpose, and an over-all inviting appearance, is in large measure due to spacing and alignment.

The degree of accuracy, time and care expended on any particular project must be determined by the ultimate purpose of the copy. Naturally, a work being prepared for publication by autograph or music typewriter methods will be given a great deal more time than one being done almost completely by hand for the main purpose of producing correct and neat copy in a minimum of time. In either case, the technical requirements are fundamentally the same, the only difference being in the over-all accuracy of forming and placing of the characters.

Whether copy is done free-hand or by more controlled methods of space measurement, one will in time develop a sense for placement on a line or page with astonishing accuracy, and the eye alone will be able to account for most of the note placement without measurement.

All manuscripts, whether of scores or parts, should be numbered in standard book fashion with even-numbered pages on the left and odd-numbered pages on the right. The beginning of a work is normally placed on an odd-numbered page. Exceptions are sometimes made for very short works or parts which take only two facing pages; in such cases the work will start on page two, rather than on page one or page three.

Any project must be planned one score line at a time. This score line may be only one staff, as for a part, or thirty staves as for a very full score; in either case, the first consideration is the equitable distribution of musical material over the width of one score line of the page.

All work must be planned to utilize the line space in such a manner as to avoid ending with an incomplete measure or having the last bar line placed at some distance from the end of the line, leaving a portion of the staff blank.

The beginning copyist may find it necessary to plan his line by lightly penciling-in note heads in their appropriate relationship to determine how many measures may be placed on the line. With experience, the number of measures can be determined by estimate, leaving any spacing adjustment to be done in the separate measures. Whatever the method may be, measure size must be set by the part having the greatest number of notes and accidentals in that measure. Obviously, a measure full of sixteenth-notes will require more space than one consisting of two half-notes, but the treatment of the problem is approached differently for a score than for a part of only one staff line. In a score, movement in another voice often makes it necessary to give disproportionate room to notes of longer duration.

When measures on a line are equal in size they may be ruled in advance of copying, marking the points with a ruler or stepping them off with the dividers. More often than not the measure lines will occur at unequal intervals, and it is a serious mistake to pre-rule a page into equal measures without careful planning and then to try to fit the work into those preset measure limits.

Measure content must be placed in such a manner that the notes are not crowded. In music manuscript too much space is far better than too little space.

Notes of equal duration should be evenly spaced. Observe the spacing of notes under each bracket in the example below.

If there are accidentals there must be allowance for additional space between notes.

Notes of varying values should be spaced in a manner to help establish the flow of the rhythm by making clear to the eye the relative durational differences.

Measure sizes in a single part can and should be suited to the musical content.

The visual factor can be important in establishing the mood or tempo of a work, especially when a performer is sight reading.

Vertical alignment of chords is always determined by the content. When all note heads are in direct vertical order there is no problem.

Chords containing the interval of a second are lined up according to the notes on the "correct" side of the stem.

Note clusters involving multiple seconds are lined up in the same manner.

Vertical placement of notes of longer duration must be accurate according to their entry in the measure. Notes having the value of a full measure are placed at the beginning of the measure, but rests of full-measure value are centered.

Where there is a key or clef change in one of the staves of a score, unequal spacing of units in the same measure on other staves is unavoidable.

Rests must be placed vertically and horizontally with the same care given to notes.

Frequently, in a fairly fast tempo, the note groupings of an uneven meter will change without a regular pattern of change. The conductor's score reading and the player's (singer's) part reading will be facilitated if, as an additional visual aid, the notes are grouped according to the beat pattern, and dotted lines are drawn between groups.

The rhythmic complexities of much contemporary music are increased if the notes of a score are cramped within measures and placed without due regard for their visual position in the time sequence. The measures must be planned in such a manner that any unusual unit divisions or rhythmic patterns will be immediately visually evident. This is especially important when no meter signatures are used.

Horizontal spacing in vocal music must take into consideration the words of the text as well as the rhythm; often a succession of short note values will need to be separated by abnormally large spaces in order to accommodate the words without crowding them.

All the words should have suf-fi-cient spac-ing

A melismatic passage, on the other hand, will not take any more space than the same note values for instruments.

A - - men. A - men. ___

The vertical alignment of the parts (i.e. the placement of beats under one another) in choral writing is not apt to have the rhythmic complexity found in instrumental music, but the same spacing principles prevail, plus the constant need to remember to leave enough room for the text.

Flutes

Oboes

Clarinets

Bassoons

I, II
Horns in F
III, IV

6

PRAIRIE SCHOONER by Anthony Donato: Copyright 1957 by The Composers Press, Inc.
Used by permission.

KEYBOARD INSTRUMENTS AND HARP

Celesta, Harp, Harpsichord, and Piano Solo. Music for these instruments is written on two staves barred together and joined further with a brace. This combination is placed at the beginning of each score line. Clef signs, key signatures, and meter signatures are placed on each staff line. Bar lines for marking measures are drawn through both staves.

Papers with braces already printed are available, with or

without clef signs, though, of course, any kind of plain staff paper may be used. The paper sizes most commonly used are approximately 9½ by 12½ inches and 11 by 13½ inches. All the various rulings and sizes are available in both opaque and transparent papers.

Titles are always centered. Tempo indications are placed above the treble staff. Dynamic signs and other performance indications are placed between the two staves unless crowding or independent staff direction makes it necessary to use space below the lower staff. Pedal marks go below the lower staff in piano music and usually between the staves in harp music.

Two Pianos, Four Hands. Music for two pianos is written in score form. The complete score serves as a performer's part, each player having a copy.

Each score line is laid out by connecting four staves together with a bar line. The upper two staves are connected with a brace and serve for the first piano part; the lower two staves are also braced and serve for the second piano part.

Bar lines are ruled only through the limits of each part, but must align for both parts. Tempo indications are placed above the top staff of each part and all performance directions must be made between the staves of each part. Pedal marks and the exceptions mentioned for piano solo go below the bass staff of each part.

Piano, Four Hands. Four-hand piano music—to be played on one piano —is composed or arranged, like two-piano music, in full score, with the higher-range notes placed on the upper score and the lower-range notes on the lower score. For parts, two methods are used. In the older method the two parts are arranged individually on facing pages in such a manner that when pages are turned, all the notes for the second player are on the left page and all the notes for the first player are on the right page. The number of measures per line on each page must correspond, since one page turn serves both players. All performance directions must be complete on each page.

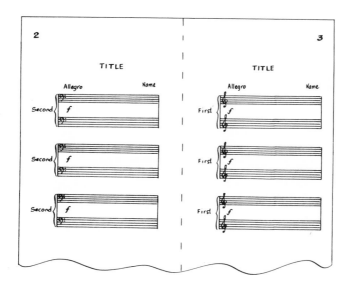

The second method simply uses the full score arrangement, with the part for the first player on the top score and that for the second player on the lower score. This arrangement has the advantage of showing each player exactly what is going on at any given moment, since both players read from the same page and the entire work is in vertical score alignment. See the example on page 102.

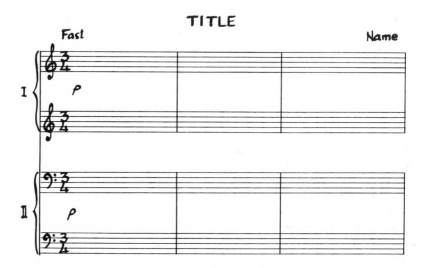

Organ. Music for organ is written on three staves, connected by a single bar line at the beginning of each score line. The upper two staves are connected with a brace and labeled *manuals,* and the lower staff is labeled *pedal.* Bar lines are ruled through the two upper staves and singly for the pedal staff.

Clef signs, key signatures, and meter signatures are placed on each staff. One tempo indication placed above the top staff serves for all three. Dynamic and other performance indications are written separately for the manuals and for the pedal; such indications for the manuals are placed between the two staves, as for piano. Performance signs for the pedal are placed beneath the staff for the left foot and above the staff for the right foot. Directions for registration are placed at the left side of the page, directly above the main tempo indication.

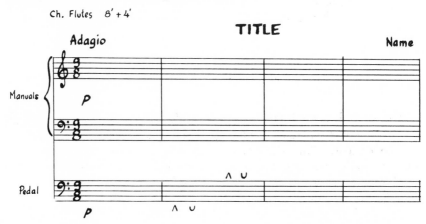

OTHER SOLO INSTRUMENTS

Unaccompanied. Parts for unaccompanied instrumental solos or those for chamber, orchestra, band or any other ensemble music, are written on any plain staff paper, available in varying page sizes and number of staves and with or without clef signs. The number of staves on a page should be determined by the space needed between staves for leger lines and for performance indications. Both opaque and transparent papers are available.

Tempo and special performance indications are placed above the staff. Dynamics and related terms and tempo change directions go below the staff.

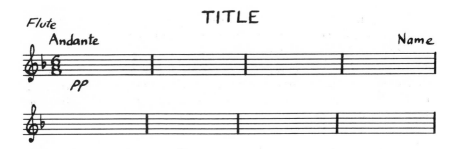

With Piano. Instrumental solos with piano accompaniment are written on three staves, one for the solo part and two for the piano. The three staves are connected with a bar line and the two piano staves are connected with a brace. Measures are ruled separately for the solo part and for the piano.

Tempo indications are placed above the solo staff and the top piano staff. Dynamics and tempo directions are written beneath the solo staff and between the two piano staves. Special performance directions for the solo part such as *con sordino*, etc., are placed above the staff.

Any blank staff paper may be used for this combination, but specially ruled papers are better suited for it, because of the increased space between the solo and piano staves, allowing more room for performance directions, thus permitting easier reading. The papers are available with or without clef signs and in both opaque and transparent types in several sizes.

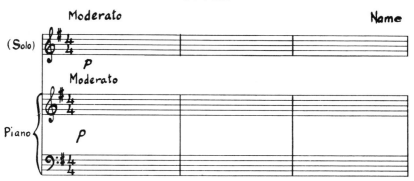

CHAMBER MUSIC WITHOUT PIANO

The page layouts for scores in this category are quite similar, especially for the most commonly used instrumental combinations.

Any blank staff paper, opaque or transparent, may be used by ruling the staves for the desired combination. There are, however, special rulings available for the more frequently-used combinations, such as trios and quartets; the beginning of each score line is already barred. For duos, the braced score lines for piano music may be used if the two instruments are alike.

For any combination, a common tempo indication will serve for all the staves when it is placed above the top staff. Dynamics and tempo change indications must be placed under each staff as needed, and special performance directions go above each staff.

Placement of instrumental staves on the score page is done according to a standard fixed order for the most-used combinations and by large-ensemble order in others. Woodwind scores follow the usual orchestra-score order of flute, oboe, clarinet, and bassoon. In woodwind quintet scores the horn part is placed above that of the bassoon, in order to have the bass clef at the bottom of the score. Brass ensemble scores follow the order of the brass section of full band scores: trumpets, horns, trombones, baritones (euphoniums), and tubas. String combinations are written in the normal order of violin, viola, cello, and bass.

In scores for mixed instrumental combinations, pitch ranges have a bearing on instrumental staff placement. In some instances treble clefs are kept above bass clefs, especially in smaller groupings. Otherwise, mixed-ensemble score order follows that of orchestra-score order: wood-winds, brass, percussion, harp, piano, and strings. In some instances percussion parts are placed at the bottom of the score.

There is some slight variation in the ruling of bar lines. For duos, trios, quartets, quintets, and sextets composed of instruments from the same choir and in most cases of mixed instrumentation, staves of each score line are connected with a bar line and a heavy bracket. Measure lines are ruled through all the staves.

Shown below are score lines for several combinations of two or more instruments.

Duos.

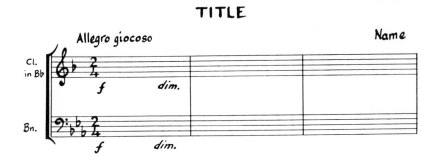

Trios.

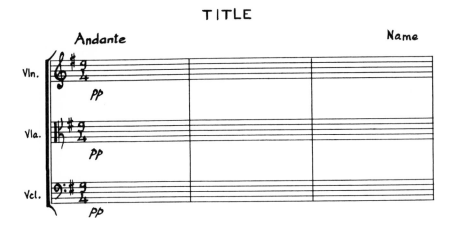

Quartets.

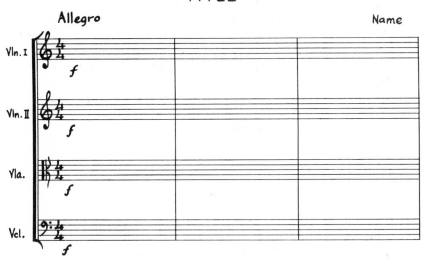

Quintets.

Sextets.

TITLE

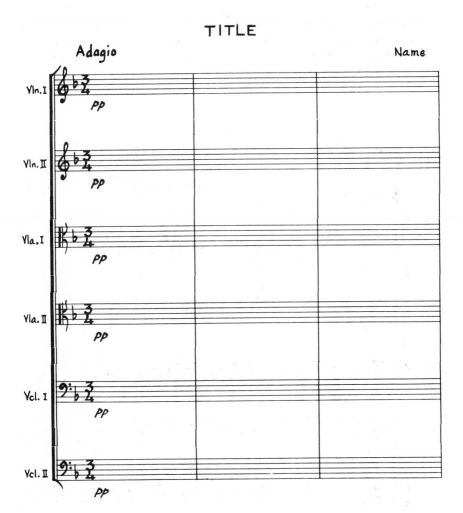

Larger Ensembles. For larger groups ruling is done either through all the staves or by choirs. The choir ruling seems to be gaining in favor. In this system all staves of each score line are connected with a bar line, and choir sections are marked with a heavy bracket at the beginning of each line; bar lines for measures are drawn only through the staves of each choir.

When the larger ensemble groups are composed of instruments of the same choir, measure barring is often done by groups of like instruments.

TITLE

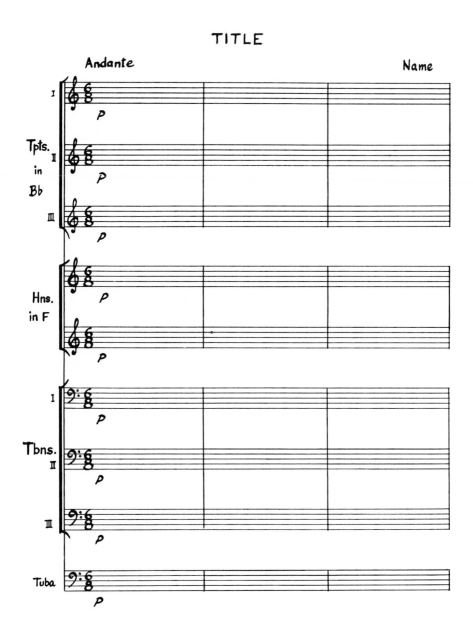

CHAMBER MUSIC WITH PIANO

Although sonatas for various instruments with piano fall into the chamber music category, the page layout is not given here because it is the same as that for solo with piano accompaniment.

Trios. For trios, traditional practice connects all the staves with a single bar line, with the customary brace for the piano. Measure lines are ruled separately for each instrument. Tempo indications are placed above the top instrumental staff and above the piano staff. Each instrumental part must have separate dynamic and performance indications.

There is a tendency today to bracket and to rule bar lines through the two instrumental staves. This seems logical, since it is customary in ensemble music without piano.

There seems to be more reason for the separate ruling when the instruments are of mixed categories; separate ruling keeps the choirs separated, as in larger ensembles.

TITLE

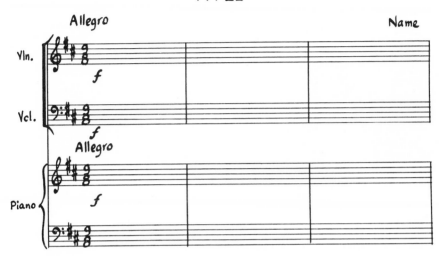

Quartets. Quartets are traditionally barred in the same manner as trios.

TITLE

Here, too, there is a tendency today to rule measure lines through all the instrumental staves, especially if the instruments are all of the same family (page 112, top).

Where the instruments are of mixed categories, bar ruling according to instrumental choirs seems logical and easy to read (page 112, bottom).

Quintets. Separate bar lines are also the traditional ruling for quintets.

As with quartets, the alternate ruling is gaining in favor.

Sextets. Traditional ruling for sextets is the same as for the other groups, though the tendency today is also for ruling through the staves. Mixed groupings are usually barred by choirs, as shown above for the mixed quartet score.

Larger Mixed Ensembles. In mixed groups, the piano is often placed in regular orchestral order with winds above and strings below the piano staff. Bar lines are ruled according to choirs.

LARGE ENSEMBLES

Orchestra. Concert orchestra layouts, regardless of size or instrumentation, are all based on an unvarying order of the instruments as they appear on the score page. Any additions or subtractions do not change this basic order.

A large major symphony orchestra has the following standard instrumentation. The instruments are listed in score order.

Piccolo
Flutes 1 and 2
Oboes 1 and 2
English Horn
Clarinets 1 and 2
Bass Clarinet
Bassoons 1 and 2
Contra Bassoon
Horns 1, 2, 3, 4
Trumpets 1, 2, 3
Trombones 1, 2, 3
Tuba
Timpani
Percussion
Harp
Piano
Celesta
Strings

Both opaque and transparent score papers are available. Plain staff papers are made with staff rulings up to thirty or more staves. If not more than twenty staves are needed the 11 by 13½ inch size papers will be adequate and make a convenient score size. For full scoring projects, however, one will probably need at least twenty-four staves, page size 11 by 15 inches. For larger instrumentation there are papers having up to thirty or more staves, page size 11 by 17 inches.

There are several paper styles that list the instruments and have the various instrumental choirs already barred. If these papers are at least approximately ruled for the work at hand they can save a great deal of copying time. Some have separate staves for Flutes I and II, Oboes I and II, etc. These should be used only if there is considerable independent movement of the parts because considerable time can be saved in unison writing for these instruments by having them share a staff, using the term a2. One should examine several different rulings and select the most suitable one. Most often one will find it necessary to do all of the choir ruling and the listing of instruments on plain staff paper. Although this is more laborious, it has the advantage of free choice of paper size and staff ruling, permitting a layout exactly suited to the need.

If the piccolo is to alternate with flute it is sometimes written below the staff for Flutes I and II. In any case, it is Flute III that alternates with the piccolo. In smaller orchestras Flute II alternates with the piccolo.

The English horn alternates with Oboe III; in smaller orchestras it alternates with Oboe II.

The bass clarinet alternates with Clarinet III if it is needed, and the contrabassoon alternates with Bassoon III. In smaller orchestras the second player alternates in each case.

For alternating instruments the direction, "change to _____," or "muta in _____," is always given above the staff as soon as possible before the point of the actual change. If the new instrument requires a change of key signature, that should be shown along with the direction for change.

Parts for the four horns are written on two staves so that Horns I and II are on the upper staff and Horns III and IV on the lower staff.

Trumpet I has a staff by itself, and Trumpets II and III share a staff.

Trombones I and II share a staff, and Trombone III, usually a bass trombone, shares a staff with the tuba, unless there is considerable independent motion in either part.

The timpani part is written on a separate staff—without any other percussion parts, unless the score is for a very small group in which one player must play all timpani and percussion parts. Percussion staves vary in number, depending on the amount of simultaneous playing of different instruments.

Divisi parts in the strings are written on the same staff unless independence of parts requires the addition of more staves. Any extended solo parts should be written on separate staves above those of the regular section.

Smaller orchestra score layouts follow the regular order, by choirs, of the instruments.

In laying out a score on plain staff paper, all of the required staves are connected with a single bar line. Complete choirs are marked off with heavy brackets and like instrument staves are joined by an additional heavy bracket or a brace. Measure lines are ruled only through complete choirs. Ruling by choirs is preferable to the older system of ruling through the complete score, because the smaller bar line groupings make instant identification of parts more certain in rapid reading.

Key signatures, if used, are placed on every staff except those for the horns and possibly those of the other transposing instruments. As we mentioned before, there is increasing tendency to dispense with all signatures in all parts.

TITLE

TITLE

Allegro

Name

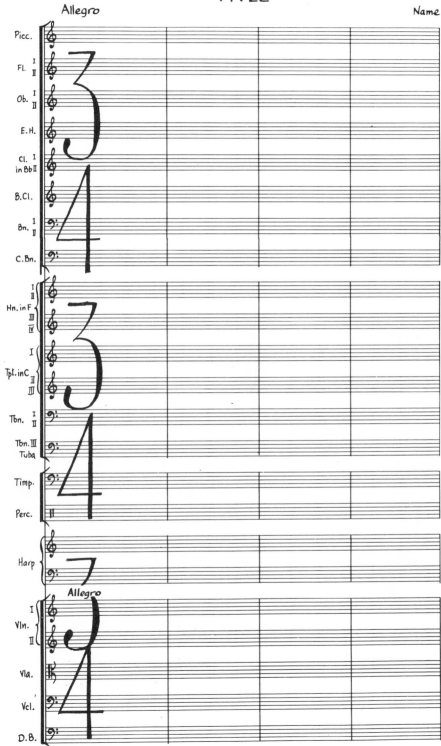

Meter signatures are traditionally placed on every staff, but there is increasing use of over-sized signatures running through several staves in order to facilitate reading for the conductor. Another method of writing meter signatures combines the traditional single staff signatures with a larger signature placed in the space immediately above the string staves.

Tempo markings are placed at the top of the score and above the Violin I staff. Dynamics go below each staff and also above a staff where they are needed because of independent motion between two instruments sharing the staff. Special performance indications go above the staves. Any instrument making an entry after the performance is under way must be given an appropriate dynamic marking.

Extended cues, written as substitute parts for missing instruments, must be shown in the full score as well as in the parts; the cued part written for the substituting instrument must be properly transposed if any transposition is involved.

Pages following the first page of a full score may be reduced by eliminating staves for instruments that are not being used if such sections are long enough to warrant the change. If, for example, only Oboe I, Horn I, Violin I, Viola, and Cello were to play for an exterded period, only five staves would need to be ruled and three lines of such scoring could be placed on one page. In manuscript there should be one or more blank staves between such score lines, adding this mark ▰ , which is placed between the scores at each end of the lines.

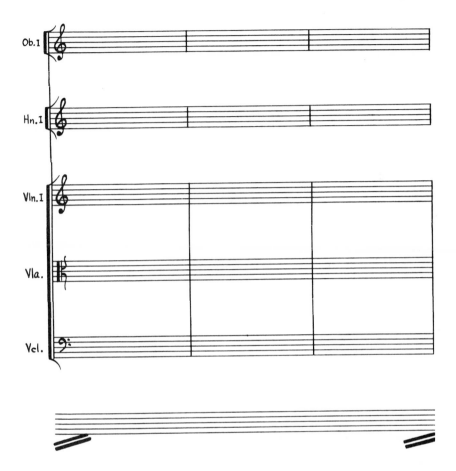

Theater Orchestra. Theater orchestras vary in size and instrumentation, but the score layout follows the regular, full-orchestra choir and instrument order, except that the piano part is placed at the bottom of the score because of its different function. This same placement for the piano part is often used for educational ensemble scores.

If saxophones are used in the score they are placed immediately below the woodwinds, above the brass section.

TITLE

Condensed Score, Orchestra. Condensed scores are used mainly for educational music and for commercial music such as shows. A sort of semi-reduced score is sometimes superposed on the regular piano part showing numerous cues arranged in such a manner that the pianist can play most of the essential parts if necessary. These are sometimes called Piano-Conductor scores.

The true fully-reduced score for large orchestras is not intended to be a piano part but is an abbreviation of the full score with all parts written in treble and bass clefs, sounding as notated. The number of staves will vary from two to four or more, depending on the complexity of the music.

In a reduced score there is usually no attempt made to show arrangement by choirs. The placement of material is made according to progress of musical ideas, with a moving melodic line on the same staff even though the instrumentation may change. Any change of instrumentation is labeled at the point of change. Doubled melodic lines and all notes of chords are labeled with the names of all instruments concerned.

Concert Band. Writing for concert band would be infinitely easier if a standard band instrumentation could be established. In spite of attempts by publishers and band societies to do this, band directors persist in making instrumental additions to or deletions from scores to suit their personal tastes or to accommodate particular local situations. To add to this confusion composers, arrangers, and publishers do not agree on exact staff placement for certain instruments. Some place the bassoons beneath the oboes, others place them under the clarinets, and still others place them below the saxophones. Baritones are found either above the trombones or directly above the tubas. The string bass part may be in the middle of the score with the contrabassoon or beneath the tubas.

The instrumentation given below is one that is widely used, and the order of instruments will at least serve as a point of departure.

Piccolo
Flutes
Oboes
E♭ clarinet
B♭ clarinets I, II, III
E♭ alto clarinet
B♭ bass clarinet
Bassoons
E♭ alto saxophones I, II
B♭ tenor saxophone
E♭ baritone saxophone
Harp ⎫
Piano ⎭ sometimes written below the percussion
B♭ cornets I, II, III
B♭ trumpets I, II
F horns I, II, III, IV
Trombones I, II, III
Baritones (euphonium)
Tubas
String bass
Timpani
Percussion

Larger bands may add the English horn, the contrabass clarinet, and the contrabassoon.

Score papers, both opaque and transparent, come in several sizes, with staff rulings ranging up to thirty or more staves. Several styles of special rulings for bands are available; one should examine them to see which, if any, is suited for any projected score. If one is usable, considerable copying time can be saved.

In ruling blank staff paper, all of the required staves are connected with a single bar line. Choirs are connected with a heavy bracket, and staves for like instruments are given an additional heavy bracket or a brace. Measure lines are ruled only through choirs.

The number of staves used depends entirely upon the amount of independent action in each part. Since a band score is, at best, a rather large affair, any sharing of staves is to be preferred if it will allow sufficient room for all musical needs. Band scores sometimes reach the point of absurdity with respect to oversized pages and number of staves used. Mere score size, unfortunately, is not necessarily a measure of quality.

TITLE

Allegro

Name

125

Key signatures are placed on every staff as needed. As with orchestra scores, however, the practice of dispensing with all key signatures is growing.

Meter signatures are traditionally placed on every staff. The use of over-sized signatures found in orchestra scores is not so frequent in band scores, but it is gaining and has much to recommend it.

Tempo markings are placed at the top of the score. Dynamics go below each staff, and where two instruments share a staff they may be needed above the staff as well. Any instrument making an entry after the performance is under way must be given an appropriate dynamic marking at the point of entry.

Reductions in portions of the full score are not possible nearly so often in band scores as they are in orchestra scores, but they can be used if lightly-scored passages are of long enough duration. If, for example, only Flutes I and II, Clarinets I and II, Horns I and II, and Trombones I and II were to play over a period taking three full score pages, staves for all instruments not playing could be eliminated and three score lines could be placed on one page. One or more staves should be left between the score lines and this mark ══ placed between the score lines at each end of the lines.

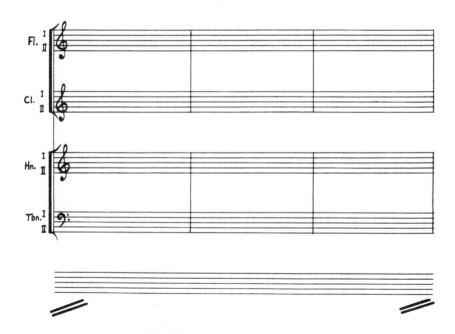

Condensed Score, Band. Condensed scores are used much more frequently for band than for orchestra. In some instances publishers issue only a condensed score. If there is a full score, publishers usually issue a condensed score as well.

The number of staves used for a condensed score will depend upon the musical content of the work. There is more tendency to show musical material by sections than in the case of the orchestral reduced score, but a continuous presentation of the musical idea is more important. All entries, doublings, and changes must be labeled as they occur. Condensed scores for band often require more staves than those for orchestra because of the larger number of instruments used in most bands.

Instrumental Solos with Large Ensembles. Layouts for instrumental solos with large ensembles are no different from those without the soloist except for the additional solo staff or staves.

In orchestra scores the solo parts are placed directly above the staves of the string section. In band scores the solo parts are placed directly above the staves of the brass section.

THE LAST SUPPER by Anthony Donato: Copyright 1958 by Southern Music Publishing Co., Inc. Used by permission.

7

PAGE LAYOUTS FOR VOCAL MUSIC

Solo songs. The paper used for songs may have any blank staff ruling, but the special type with score lines ruled for solo and piano is to be preferred, the extra spacing between the solo and piano staves allowing more room for the text.

The beginning of each score line should have a bar line connecting the vocal staff with the double staff of the piano accompaniment. The piano part receives the customary brace joining the two staves. On the special solo with piano papers this ruling is already done at the beginning of each score line.

Measure lines are ruled separately for the voice and piano parts.

All performance indications for the voice part are made above the staff in order not to conflict with the text. Performance directions for the piano part are placed between the two staves, except for tempo indications, which are placed above the top staff.

The name of the author of the poem or the text should appear at the top left side of the first page of the song. Any credit line acknowledging permission for use as given by the publisher or author of the text is to be placed at the bottom center of the first page.

Most songs are written for high, medium, or low voice, without any specific indication of voice, unless the text or style of the song makes it seem exclusively suited for a particular voice. Songs for a man's low voice range are usually less likely to have double use and are often written in the bass clef.

THE HEROES

Choral Music. Just as for solo songs, any blank staff paper may be used, but for practical use the octavo-size sheets are to be preferred, since they are handled with greater ease by singers in massed ensemble.

Each vocal part has a staff, with the highest at the top of the score. The beginning of each score line should have a double bar connecting the staves of the complete ensemble. Measure lines are drawn separately in each part in order not to interfere with the text. A piano accompaniment or rehearsal reduction part is connected to the vocal score by a single line, and the piano part has the customary brace.

All performance indications for the vocal parts are to be made above the staves, and those for piano accompaniment are placed between the two piano staves, except for the tempo indication.

The name of the author of the poem or text is placed at the top left side of the first page of the composition. Acknowledgment of permission by the author or publisher for use of the text appears at the bottom center of the first page.

Each vocal part should have its own text. However, in strictly homophonic or chordal parts, if copying time is limited, two lines of text for three or four parts can be sufficient.

Clef signs for tenor parts vary. The most common procedure is to use a regular treble clef sign for the tenor part, since there is a general understanding that the tenor part sounds an octave lower than written.

Occasionally one will see a small figure 8 attached to the lower part of the treble clef sign to indicate the octave transposition for the tenor part ♪.

A third method is the use of two treble clef signs on each tenor staff line ♪. This seems to be needlessly cumbersome.

The practice of placing a C clef 𝄡 sign on the third space is not to be recommended.

Shown below is the beginning of a composition for *a cappella* choir, SATB. Note that in this case the vocal parts are reduced to a score for rehearsal purposes. Such a reduction is customary for all unaccompanied vocal ensemble music. This reduction, of course, is eliminated if the work has an independent accompaniment.

Other voice combinations are laid out in the same manner as that for SATB. If they are unaccompanied, the rehearsal reduction is required for any choral combination of more than two parts.

PRAISE YE

Occasionally one will see soprano and alto parts on one staff and tenor and bass parts on another staff, in the bass clef. This doubling of parts is done to save space, but may be done only where there is simultaneous motion in the voices.

Such an arrangement is standard for hymns intended for congregational singing. In these there is only one text line printed between the two staves.

Division of voices within a section may be done on the same staff if the divided parts move simultaneously in rhythm and text. Where there is independence of motion and text, each part of the division requires a separate staff.

Short incidental solo parts that occur within any voice, while the other singers of the same voice are silent, may be written in the normal score position for that voice. Where the other members of the section are also singing, it will be necessary to use an extra staff for the solo part. Any extended, special solo parts must be written on a special staff placed above the staves of the regular choir.

Voice with Small Chamber Ensemble. Score arrangement for solo voice or chorus with small combinations of instruments depends on the instrumentation. Where the instruments are all of one family, the voice parts are placed above the instrumental staves. In mixed instrumentation using strings, the voice parts are placed immediately above the strings. Where the combination is woodwinds and brass, the voice parts are placed above the brass.

The beginning of each score line has a bar line connecting all of the staves and a heavy bracket to mark each instrumental choir and vocal section. Measure lines are ruled only through the instrumental choirs and the individual voice staves.

Tempo indications are placed at the top left side of the score above the top staff and above the top staff of the vocal part. Dynamic marks and performance indications go below the staves for the instruments and above the staves for the voice parts.

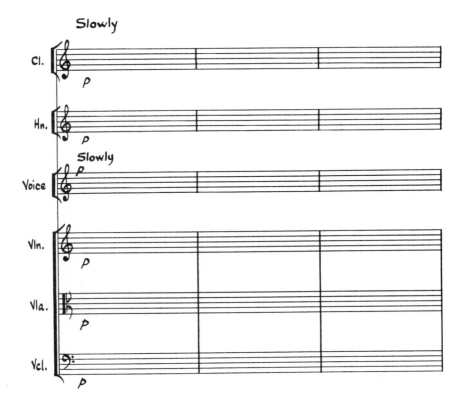

Voice with Large Ensemble. Vocal parts in large orchestral scores are placed immediately above the strings. Vocal parts in band scores are placed between the woodwind and the brass sections.

Tempo indications are placed at the top left side of the score and above the vocal part. All other placing of dynamic marks and performance indications follows the usual procedures: below the staff for instruments and above the staff for vocal parts.

Trumpet II

Prairie Schooner

Anthony Donato

Fast, with crisp vigor (♩=138)

EXTRACTING PARTS

E VERY EXPERIENCED COMPOSER or arranger knows the value
of good parts. Performers who must struggle with the
uncertainties imposed by poorly prepared parts are not
able to feel as kindly toward a work as they do when
manuscript is well organized in regard to its notation, spacing,
and general planning.

Since works for piano, two pianos, organ, solo voice, and
chorus do not have parts aside from the actual score, our re-

marks are directed toward extraction of instrumental parts for instruments not mentioned above.

The first consideration for a good part is the paper size and staff ruling.
The most popular sizes for parts for solos, chamber music, orchestra, and
band are 9½ by 12½ inches and 11 by 13½ inches, ruled with twelve staves.
The staff ruling of these sizes permits note heads of reasonable size, and
the space between staves allows enough room for performance directions,
except for those parts which consistently require large numbers of leger
lines; for these, ten-stave paper is better.

For marching bands there is a special small size measuring 5½ by 6
inches which is designed for the music clips on instruments.

Opaque and transparent papers are available in several sizes, with a
broad selection of staff rulings. There is considerable difference in staff
size and spacing between staves in papers of different manufacturers that
have the same number of staves and identical sheet sizes. One should
investigate to find the paper that best suits one's needs and tastes.

The title of a work goes at the top of the page, centered. The name of
the composer or arranger is placed at the right, just above the top staff and
the tempo indication to the left above the top staff. For an instrumental
part, the name of the instrument is placed a short distance directly above
the tempo indication.

Planning is extremely important, and the notation practices of Chapters
3 and 4 should be carefully observed. Measure sizes must be determined
by the musical content, not by arbitrary pre-ruling. It should be obvious
that a measure of $\frac{4}{4}$ meter composed largely of sixteenth-notes will require more space on the staff than a measure consisting of four quarter-
notes. Careful planning will avoid short lines or crowded last measures
of lines. With care and a little experience one will be able to judge measure space requirements with surprising accuracy.

Where the measure content is uniform and measure sizes are the same
for an extended period of time, dividers will be useful in stepping off
equal staff divisions rapidly.

There is no virtue in under-sized note heads, no matter how neat the
appearance may be. Note heads should fit into the space between two
staff lines of the paper being used.

Each player should have his own part. If the score shows, for example,
Flutes I and II on one staff, separate parts should be extracted for each
player.

Timpani parts are normally separate from percussion parts. In chamber
orchestras, however, there may be only one player to play all timpani and
percussion parts. In that case it is necessary to write the timpani part on

one staff and all other percussion parts on another, with the two barred together.

Regular percussion parts are arranged in various ways. If the parts in the score are written on several lines with specific instruments for each line, the parts are copied in the same manner. Where there is considerable, though not necessarily simultaneous, percussion activity, the division of labor is best left to the players, since different ensembles have different practices for sharing the work in the percussion section. If two, three, or more lines of percussion are indicated, all of them should be copied onto one part; by making duplicate parts, players of any ensemble can divide the work according to their own practice or convenience if specific instruments for each player are not indicated.

Rehearsal points in all ensemble music are absolutely mandatory. The choice between rehearsal numbers or letters is optional, and each system has some merit. For ease of checking parts with the score the numbers are definitely easier to use. As for frequency, numbering measures in multiples of ten seems to be the most convenient number for most purposes.

In placing either rehearsal numbers or letters, one will often find the point occurring during a rest period for some instrument. In such a case it becomes necessary to show the rehearsal point accurately by making a division of the rest. For example, the oboe has twelve measures of rest, and the rehearsal number 30 falls within this period. One rest with "12" written over it does not give adequate information to the player regarding the exact point of the rehearsal number. Assuming that the rehearsal number comes after seven measures of rest for the oboe, the part should be written as below.

One of the most important considerations for all parts is the problem of page turns. The part should always be planned in such a way that the turn comes, if possible, at a rest point. If this means leaving three or four blank staves on the page, by all means, leave them blank. Turns in the middle of a passage simply cannot be negotiated except in some instances of an open string or of a held note requiring only one hand on an instrument. String parts in orchestra music are not as critical as single-player ensemble parts, because one player at each stand can turn the page while the other continues playing. However, there is a weakening of the sound that may be disastrous in an especially difficult passage. Turning pages on rest points in string parts is also highly desirable.

Where the part is relatively short, the turn problem may sometimes be solved by writing the part on facing pages, eliminating the turn.

The matter of page numbering is closely related to turning points. Normally, all new work begins on the right, or odd-numbered page. This means that all turns come on odd-numbered pages, and it is extremely important that the work is printed correctly with odd-numbered pages on the right side. The exception of parts on facing pages requires starting the part on the left page, that is, number two.

Page numbers are equally correct when placed at top center, bottom center, or in outside top corners. The corner placing has the advantage of guaranteeing correct positioning for any printing, since any accidental opposite placement would position the page numbers in the inside corners and on the wrong sides.

Where the rest period for any player is exceptionally long, or where the music is particularly complex, cue notes are exceedingly helpful for assuring correct entry. There is no definite number of measures of rest that marks the need for cue notes; this is determined by the character of the music.

Any cue selected to aid in entry should be one that is easily heard by the player at rest. In many cases it may be the most prominent melodic line, but it need not necessarily be that; it might well be activity of immediately surrounding players. For example, if Trombone III has been resting for thirty-five measures and is to be cued for entry, the cue might be a slightly earlier entry of Trombones I and II if they, too, had been silent for a period.

Two types of cue are shown below.

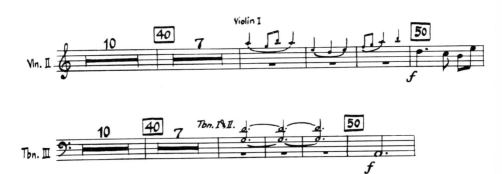

Cues written into parts for transposing instruments should be transposed to the correct notation for the instrument concerned. For example, an oboe part being written as a cue into a clarinet part should be notated as the clarinet player would see it to produce the same pitches. A treble clef cue written into a bass clef part necessitates a change of clef for the cue and another change back to the bass clef at the point of entry.

PRAIRIE SCHOONER by Anthony Donato: Copyright 1957 by The Composers Press, Inc.
Used by permission.

9

REPRODUCTION AND BINDING

REPRODUCTION

THE DEVELOPMENT of modern duplicating methods has been a boon beyond price to anyone needing manuscript copies of any kind. The drudgery of making multiple copies by hand or of having to resort to the limited and inordinately expensive duplicating processes of a few years ago has been completely eliminated. A duplicating process to take care of just about any contingency is available to anyone who needs it, either locally or through mail-order services.

143

Most composers and arrangers, student or professional, and teachers and students concerned with any kind of manuscript reproduction are primarily interested in having only a small number of copies of a work; there may be an occasional need for the duplication of fifty or a hundred copies. Some duplication processes are admirably suited to turning out copies in small numbers, whereas others are better suited to quantity reproduction. This chapter deals briefly with some of the systems used for duplication of music manuscript and compares some of the advantages and disadvantages of each.

Diazo Process. Probably the most common method for the reproduction of music manuscript in relatively small quantities is by the *diazo* process, often known as the *black and white,* or *B. and W.,* process. Basically a light-sensitive paper and ammonia vapor process, its use for music reproduction has evolved from blueprint processes used by commercial firms doing work for architects, draftsmen, and others. Most cities have at least one such firm that will do music work, and several specialists in music reproduction are known nationally and do a large volume of mail-order business. The process itself has improved in recent years, and the net result is much cleaner and whiter copy, the gray-green cast of the earlier days having largely disappeared. It is possible to get nearly perfect black on white prints, and one should not be satisfied with inferior work. There is some tendency toward discoloration with age, but the improvement in this respect, too, has been marked. On the whole, it is a very satisfactory method for small-scale reproduction because of its availability and relatively low cost.

The paper on which the music to be reproduced must be written is often called transparent, but is actually translucent. It is also referred to as onion skin. It comes in many sheet sizes with a variety of staff rulings and may be purchased in music stores or directly from firms specializing in music reproduction. Today most staff rulings are on the back of the sheet, permitting the erasure of mistakes without ruining the staff.

It is absolutely essential to make any copy on such papers with heavy ink (see Chapter 2). Most water inks, such as those used for fountain pens, will not reproduce too well in light lines, such as note stems. Any typewritten material must be typed with the back of the sheet in direct contact with the carbon side of a carbon sheet so that reproduced characters be equal in darkness to those made with ink. A good way to check opacity of completed work is to hold the sheet toward a window or a bright light with the inked side facing the light; if the work looks uniformly dark it will reproduce well.

The translucent manuscript sheet is the actual master for reproduction which is run through a machine that makes direct exposure on sensitized paper exposed to a light. It is then chemically fixed, or set. Prints may be made in reasonably large quantities as long as the master sheet is good. The cost of printing is determined by the page size; single-page prices vary from nine to fourteen cents per page for an 11 × 14-inch size. Printing on both sides of a sheet, known as Duplex, is preferable to single-side printing because it requires less bulk for large scores and eliminates the need for accordion folding or for pasting the pages together. It is important that all master sheets used for any particular work have the same size, staff ruling, and manufacturer, because any variation in opacity will result in prints of unequal darkness, since the machine is set before a printing to accommodate the exposure needs of that particular run.

Diazo process machines are frequently used for office duplication needs. If one has access to such a machine, one may be able to do one's own reproduction at very small cost.

Spirit Duplicators. One of the oldest methods for office duplication is the *spirit duplication* process. The machines, sold under various trade names, are common in business offices and educational institutions and afford a means for making a moderate number of copies at small cost. Master sheets, which cost from five to ten cents each, will print a page size of 8½ × 11 inches. Music sheets with a variety of staff rulings are obtainable.

The paper master sheets come with a carbon sheet attached to the back. After the music is written on the ruled staves with an ordinary pencil or by music typewriter, the carbon back is removed, and the prepared sheet is run through the duplicator. The color of the reproduced work varies from purple to black. Prints have a tendency to fade, although there has been great improvement in this respect.

The spirit process is best suited for classroom assignments or for duplication of work intended for temporary or emergency use. The printing is done on ordinary paper and is possible on both sides of a sheet, although it has a tendency to show through.

Photocopy, Thermography, and the Electrostatic Process. The development of machines for office copy use has been almost phenomenal in recent years. While they are intended mainly for duplication of office records, correspondence, and other business needs, they can reproduce music manuscript perfectly if they are large enough to accommodate music-size sheets. Most of them will take a sheet eleven inches wide. Length is no problem since reproduction papers may be ordered in any desired length. Printing on both sides of the sheet is possible with Duplex papers.

One of the chief virtues of these machines is their ability to reproduce virtually anything printed or written, as long as it is on a flat, detached sheet and can be introduced into the machine. This means that they can reproduce music manuscript that is written on either opaque or translucent paper.

There are several different processes used in these machines, aside from the diazo process mentioned earlier. *Photocopy* makes use of two processes, diffusion and dye transfer, both based on photographic principles. In the *diffusion* process copies are made by direct contact with a sensitized negative paper, the image then being transferred to a specially treated positive sheet. This is sometimes a two-step process, but it is quite fast. The *dye transfer* process uses a coated matrix in place of the negative paper and transfers the image to ordinary, non-coated paper. Three or four good copies can be made from this matrix. Costs for either process will run from six to eleven cents per single-page copy.

Thermography utilizes a heat-sensitive process which transfers the desired image to sensitized copy paper that is exposed to infra-red light. Copy costs are approximately the same as for photocopy.

The *electrostatic* process is newer for desk-type machines but may prove to be one of the most versatile. The image is produced by use of an electrical charge and without liquids. Single-copy costs are approximately the same as for the other processes. One of the advantages is that any page copy made by this machine can be used as an offset master for quantity production in an offset printing machine.

Offset Printing. Offset printing machines can produce fine quality printing in large quantities, and it is precisely this for which they are best suited. The cost for quantity printing is very low. The machines come under various trade names and are often used in schools and business offices.

Masters may be of several types, but the kind that is of greatest interest to those who want music reproduction in rather modest quantities is a special kind of paper on which the writing is done with a special pencil or with typewriters and music typewriters equipped with ribbons made for the purpose. Paper of this kind, with any desired staff rulings, can be made up on order by the manufacturers. These paper masters will produce copies in large quantities on ordinary paper at small cost and may be kept for future use. Printing can be done on both sides of a sheet.

A composer with access to an offset machine is able to duplicate choral or instrumental parts at very low cost. Blank master sheets cost approximately eleven cents each and will print on any kind of regular paper including a 9½ × 12½-inch size well suited for instrumental parts.

Photostatic Printing. The photostatic process consists of making a photographic negative of the work to be duplicated. Any number of positive prints can be made from this negative in any size with perfect reproduction. The process is particularly useful for duplicating pages in bound volumes or scores that cannot be removed for duplication by photocopy or similar means. Reproduction by the photostatic process is rather expensive and is not often used for routine music duplication.

Xerography. Xerography is an electrostatic process that is useful in several ways. In addition to producing duplicates in the ordinary manner it is used for making master sheets for use in printing by offset machines or spirit duplicators or for making translucent masters for the diazo process. The cost per page varies according to the kind of master sheet that is prepared.

There are several firms in various parts of the country that specialize in music reproduction. Most of them are equipped to duplicate manuscript by more than one means, but the most-used method is the diazo process. They are also able to supply the translucent master sheets with a variety of staff rulings.

The chief advantage of firms specializing in music reproduction is their fixed prices per page—other sources may be more expensive. Also, these firms are able to supply at least one form of binding at a reasonable cost. There is, of course, great convenience in doing business at home and one should investigate the local resources to determine what services, if any, are available.

Reproduction by various methods is available in every city of moderate size, and though not all firms are especially equipped to do the best music work, most of them can at least take care of an emergency, such as the loss of a part.

BINDING

Any music reproduction of more than one sheet presents the problem of binding, both for convenience and for security in performance. Scores or parts submitted for reading or performance in loose sheets are an invitation to trouble.

Most firms specializing in music reproduction have at least one kind of binding service and some offer several. If there are not too many sheets to be bound, or if one owns or has access to binding equipment, it may be possible to do satisfactory work at home.

Accordion Fold. One of the simplest means for attaching sheets together is the accordion fold method. Accordion folding can be done only when the music pages are printed on a continuous paper strip and on only one side. It was used extensively in the early days of music reproduction by the diazo method but has almost disappeared today because of the popularity of Duplex papers. The person using this technique should make certain that the printed sheets are pasted together at least at the hinge edges; an accordion fold of twenty or so loose pages that is dropped in performance makes quite an impressive catastrophe.

Stapling and Saddle Stitching. Stapling is a very inexpensive and simple method of binding that is often used for instrumental parts, songs, or any work having a relatively small number of pages. This method requires that the printing be on both sides of the sheets, two pages on each side, and will accommodate not more than a total of thirty to forty pages; that is, fifteen to twenty folded sheets. The main difficulty created by this form of binding is getting the pages to lie flat on a music stand, although for the average part running from six to twelve pages the fault is not too serious.

Saddle stitching is exactly the same as stapling except that the sheets are sewn through with thread or cord rather than stapled.

Stapling single sheets together through their page margins is possible for works that do not need to lie flat or stay open and where there are not too many sheets to be fastened. This method, which is fairly satisfactory for hand-held choral parts, should never be used for scores or instrumental parts.

Plastic Ring and Wire Spiral. Plastic ring binding and wire spiral binding are the two methods most often used for scores whose maximum thickness (bulk) is one and one-quarter inches, including the covers, which may be either flexible or stiff. Most duplicating firms can supply one or both types at quite reasonable cost. Binding machines may be purchased for home or office.

Cloth Tape. Cloth tape binding, one of the most satisfactory methods, is not often offered by duplicating firms although one Chicago area firm, the Kayser Music Binding Co., furnishes it as a part of the reproduction service. The well-known Gamble Hinge binding is one of the few available as a binding service; it costs from three to five cents per sheet for the service. Also, the tape is sold for home or office use and may be purchased from a music dealer. There are other gummed tapes on the market, some of them in multi-hinged form similar to that of the Gamble Hinge. They can be purchased at most office supply stores.

It is not advisable to try multiple-sheet cloth tape binding without proper equipment.

Unless one does one's own binding it is best to have binding done along with reproduction. Having manuscripts duplicated at one place and bound at another is usually more expensive than the combined service.

Some firms that specialize in music reproduction and binding that have established nationally known service are listed below. These are by no means the only firms that give satisfactory reproduction service; the list is given as an aid to those who have no local facilities or may not know where to turn.

Papers, Reproduction, and Binding

> Al Boss Music Reproduction
> 2018 Walnut Street
> Philadelphia 3, Pa.
>
> Cameo Music Reproduction
> 1527½ North Vine Street
> Hollywood 28, Calif.
>
> Circle Blue Print Co.
> 225 West 57th Street
> New York 19, N. Y.
>
> Independent Music Publishers
> 215 East 42nd Street
> New York 17, N. Y.
>
> National Blue Print Co.
> 110 West 32nd Street
> New York 1, N. Y.

Reproduction and Binding only:

> Kayser Music Binding Co.
> 1022 11th Street
> Wilmette, Ill.
>
> Rochester Photo Copy
> 887 Portland Ave.
> Rochester 21, N. Y.

PROOFREADING

ALL MANUSCRIPT WORK of any kind should be carefully checked before it is submitted to anyone for performance. Perfect, errorless copy is rare, but it is a goal worth attempting. Remember that any mistakes appearing in work that is reproduced are compounded and corrections become increasingly difficult. The time spent on making corrections before reproduction is actually time gained.

There is no substitute for patient, careful reading of every

Standard Proofreader's Signs

Standard proofreader's signs may be used for correcting any verbal material; some of the signs may be applied to the correction of music as well. The following table shows commonly used proofreader's signs:

ℒ͗	Delete	⊙	Insert colon
ℒ͗	Delete and close up	;/	Insert semicolon
⌒	Ligature i.e., a e print æ	⋏ or ,/	Insert comma
⌣	Close up	∨/	Insert apostrophe
℘	Turn reversed letter	∨͗/	Insert quotation marks
∧	Insert (caret)	=/	Insert hyphen
#	Space	_wf_	Wrong font Character wrong size or style
∟ or ⊏	Move to left	_ital_	Set in italic type—in margin, with text underlined
⅃ or ⊐	Move to right	_rom._	Set in Roman type Text should be circled
⌐⌐	Elevate	_bf_	Set in boldface type Wavy ⌇⌇ line under text
⌊⌋	Lower	⌒ _tr_	Transpose Transpose—marginal notation
⅟͞m	One-em dash	_s c._	Small capitals Double line drawn under text ═
/| or //	Straighten ends of lines	_caps_	Capitals Triple line drawn under text ≡
══	Align, i.e., A̲l̲i̲g̲n̲	_ld_	Insert lead between lines
⌣	Push down a space	_l.c._	Lower case
X	Broken type	_stet_	Restore words crossed out Dotted line . . . written under words to be kept
�	New paragraph		
_no_ �	No paragraph		
(SP)	Spell out		
⊙	Insert period		

measure of every part. Very often a composer will proofread a part with a sort of semi-concentration that overlooks certain errors simply because the musical mind reads what should be there rather than what is actually seen by the eye.

Errors by the engraver or the autographer are also possible in work being prepared for publication. Many of the mistakes are minor ones such as omission of a flag on a note stem or an incomplete phrasing slur. An additional hazard is the fact that the proofs of work being made ready for publication are often printed with white notes and symbols on a light green background making it more difficult to find mistakes.

Proofreading of work prepared by autography or music typewriter requires extremely careful handling, because the pages being corrected will be photoengraved and must be kept clean and undamaged. Corrections made on work of this kind must be made very lightly with a light blue pencil; such marks will not show in the photographic transfer.

Page sizes of works prepared in this manner are usually over-sized and are reduced to standard dimensions in the photographic process.

For music corrections not covered by this table one should use music signs and symbols.

All corrections, whether made with standard signs or music symbols, must be shown in the margins of the page with leader lines drawn to the exact point of each correction. Sometimes it is helpful to circle the correction at the end of the leader line. If a symbol or a verbal direction is missing, it must be written in the desired place and a leader line extended from it to the nearest margin space with the correction repeated in the margin. Note corrections are best shown by circling the wrong note, extending a leader line to a margin point opposite the staff concerned and drawing a small staff with the correction made therein.

The example on page 150 shows many errors with correction marks drawn in the margins as they might appear on copy returned to a publisher. Slight variations in signs and their use are, of course, to be expected.

The Paint Box

Anthony Donato

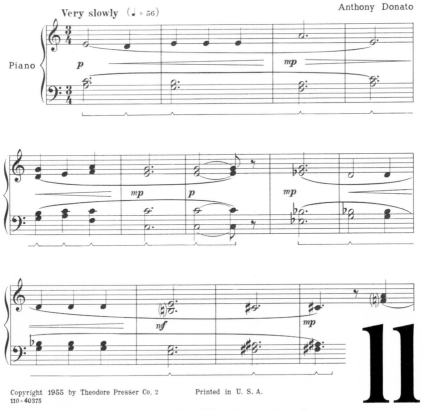

11

COPYRIGHT

Acopyright is a form of protection. In music, it may apply to a completely original composition, to an arrangement, or to a new version of an earlier work. A copyright may cover a work that is entirely music or a musical work with a text such as a song, a choral work, or an opera.

The owner of a copyright to a work has exclusive rights to copy the work, sell or distribute it in any way, or to revise or arrange it in a new form. He also has performance rights limited to those performances for profit and the right to make the first sound recording of the work.

The advisability of securing a copyright must be determined by individual circumstances. Works that are to be published for sale by a commercial publisher are ordinarily copyrighted in the name of the firm; if the work in question has previously been copyrighted by the composer the copyright is assigned to the publisher and recorded in his name.

Publication does not necessarily mean the sale of commercially printed copies of a work; the term applies also to wide and unrestricted distribution of a work in any form of reproduction other than sound media, such as phonograph records and tapes. The distribution may be either gratis or by sale.

Limited distribution of copies of a work for use by performers, or for submission to publishers, conductors, or contests does not constitute publication, nor does performance of a work.

Unpublished works are protected by Common Law right without the securing of a copyright. Such protection ends, however, if the work is published in any way and it becomes available for use by anyone without restriction. This is known as being in *public domain.*

Copyright for an unpublished work is especially desirable if it is to be recorded; technically, recording is not publication, but it will have wide distribution and probably should have the protection of a copyright.

In order to get protection for an unpublished work beyond that afforded by the Common Law right it is necessary to obtain statutory copyright by registering a claim in the Copyright Office in Washington, D. C. The procedure is quite simple. For musical compositions it is necessary to make an application to the Copyright Office on Form E, intended especially for musical compositions. These forms are available from the Copyright Office without charge. The completed form, together with one copy of the work to be registered and a check, bank draft, or money order for the registration fee of $4.00 made out to the Register of Copyrights, should be sent to the Register of Copyrights, The Library of Congress, Washington 25, D. C.

Copyright protection on the work begins on the date the registration is made and is in force for a period of twenty-eight years from that date. The copyright may be renewed for a second term of twenty-eight years by making an application for renewal during the last year of the first twenty-eight-year term. The renewal application is made on Form R, and the renewal fee is $2.00.

Statutory copyright on a work published for sale by a commercial publisher, as mentioned earlier, is normally obtained by the publisher and in the name of the firm. The procedure for obtaining such copyright registration is the same, however, for anyone, and a composer or arranger who wants to publish his own works would need to re-register his work, if it is already registered as an unpublished work, by following the procedure for registry of published works.

In order to secure a copyright for either a new registration for a published work or for a previously registered unpublished work it is first necessary to print or reproduce it, making certain that each copy contains a copyright notice in the correct place. The first part of such a notice consists of the word "Copyright," the abbreviation "Copr.," or the symbol "©." The second part of the notice consists of the year date of publication, which means the year in which copies of the work are first published in any way. If the work has already been registered for copyright in unpublished form the notice should contain the year date of the previous registration. The third part of the notice consists of the name of the copyright owner. The three parts of the notice must appear together on the title page or the first page of music in this manner:

© 1963 John Blank

After placing copies of the work on sale or making public distribution, two copies, along with a properly completed application on Form E, plus a check, or bank draft, or a money order for the registration fee of $4.00 made out to the Register of Copyrights, should be sent to the Register of Copyrights, The Library of Congress, Washington 25, D. C.

Any protective rights in a registered unpublished work will be irrevocably lost if there is publication of the work without the required statutory copyright notice on each copy, as required for published works.

The copyright term for a published work is twenty-eight years from the date of publication with notice of copyright unless the work has been previously registered in unpublished form. In that case, the term is twenty-eight years from the date of the first registration. The copyright may be renewed for another twenty-eight year period by making an application for renewal on Form R during the last year of the first twenty-eight-year term.

The owner of a copyright has the exclusive right to make or license the first sound recording of the work. As soon as it is recorded or licensed for recording it is necessary to submit special Form U to the Register of Copyrights, along with a fee of $2.00.

Detailed information concerning all aspects of copyright is available from government offices in Washington. Some of the publications that are of interest to composers and arrangers are listed on page 158.

Copyright Law of the United States of America, Bulletin No. 14, 25 cents. Available from the Superintendent of Documents, U.S. Government Printing Office, Washington 25, D. C.

The following publications are all available from the Register of Copyrights, The Library of Congress, Washington 25, D. C., free of charge.

The Copyright Office of the United States of America.
General Information on Copyright. Circular No. 35.
Notice of Use of Music. Circular No. 5.
Musical Compositions. Circular No. 58.
Song Lyrics. Circular No. 67.
Application blank, Form E, Musical Composition.
Application blank, Form D, Dramatico-Musical Composition.
Application blank, Form R, Renewal copyright.
Application blank, Form U, Notice of use of Musical composition on Mechanical instruments.

APPENDIX

DEGREES OF THE SCALE

English	Italian	French	German
Major	Maggiore	Majeur	Dur
Minor	Minore	Mineur	Moll
C flat	Do bemolle	Ut (Do) bémol	Ces
C	Do	Ut (Do)	C
C sharp	Do diesis	Ut (Do) dièze	Cis
D flat	Re bemolle	Re bémol	Des
D	Re	Re	D
D sharp	Re diesis	Re dièze	Dis
E flat	Mi bemolle	Mi bémol	Es
E	Mi	Mi	E
E sharp	Mi diesis	Mi dièze	Eis
F flat	Fa bemolle	Fa bémol	Fes
F	Fa	Fa	F
F sharp	Fa diesis	Fa dièze	Fis
G flat	Sol bemolle	Sol bémol	Ges
G	Sol	Sol	G
G sharp	Sol diesis	Sol dièze	Gis
A flat	La bemolle	La bémol	As
A	La	La	A
A sharp	La diesis	La dièze	Ais
B flat	Si bemolle	Si bémol	B
B	Si	Si	H
B sharp	Si diesis	Si dièze	His

NAMES OF INSTRUMENTS AND VOICES
WITH ABBREVIATIONS

The instruments listed here are those used in both band and orchestra scores and are not necessarily in exact score order for either group. For correct order of instruments refer to page 124 for band and to page 116 for orchestra.

Many of the instruments have optional names and abbreviations. The names in this table are the most widely used, and the abbreviations are the shortest or the best-known.

English	Italian	French	German
		WOODWINDS	
Piccolo (Picc.)	Flauto piccolo or Ottavino (Picc.)	Petite Flûte (Pte Fl.)	Kleine Flöte (Kl. Fl.)
Flute(s) (Fl.)	Flauto(-i) (Fl.)	Grande(s) Flûte(s) (Gde Fl.)	Grosse Flöte(n) (Fl.)
Alto Flute (in G) (Alto Fl.)	Flauto contralto (Fl. c'alto)	Flûte alto (en sol) (Fl. alto)	Altflöte (Altfl.)
Oboe(s) (Ob.)	Oboe(-i) (Ob.)	Hautbois (Hb.)	Hoboe(n) (Hob.)
English Horn (E. H.)	Corno inglese (Cor. ingl.)	Cor Anglais (Cor. Ang.)	Englisch Horn (Engl. Hr.)
Eb Clarinet (Eb Cl.)	Clarinetto piccolo in Mib (Cl. picc.)	Petite clarinette en Mib (Pte Cl.)	Klarinette in Es (Es-Kl.)
Clarinet(s) (Cl.)	Clarinetto(-i) (Cl.)	Clarinette(s) (Cl.)	Klarinette(n) (Kl.)
Alto Clarinet (Alto Cl.)	Clarinetto contralto (Cl. c'alto)	Clarinette alto (Cl. alto)	Altklarinette (Altkl.)
Bass Clarinet (B. Cl.)	Clarinetto basso (Cl. b.)	Clarinette basse (Cl. B.)	Bassklarinette (Basskl.)
Contrabass Clarinet (Cb. Cl.)	Clarinetto contrabasso (Cl. Cb.)	Clarinette contrebasse (Cl. C. B.)	Kontrabass Klarinette (Kb. Kl.)
Bassoon(s) (Bn.)	Fagotto(-i) (Fg.)	Basson(s) (Bon)	Fagott(e) (Fg.)
Contra or Double Bassoon (C. or D. Bn.)	Contrafagotto (C. fg.)	Contrebasson (C. Bon)	Kontrafagott (Kfg.)
Saxophone(s) (Sax.)	Sassofono(-i) (Sass.)	Saxophone(s) (Sax.)	Saxophon(e) (Sax.)

English	Italian	French	German
		BRASSES	
Horn(s) (Hn.)	Corno(-i) (Cor.)	Cor(s)	Horn (Hörner) (Hrn.)
Trumpet(s) (Tpt.)	Tromba(-e) (Tr.)	Trompette(s) (Tr.)	Trompete(n) (Tr.)
Cornet(s) (Cnt.)	Cornetto(-i) a pistoni (C.-a-p.)	Cornet(s)- à-pistons (C.-à-p.)	**Cornett(e)** (Cor.)
Bass Trumpet (B. Tpt.)	Tromba bassa (Tr. bassa)	Trompette basse (**Tr. basse**)	Basstrompete (Basstr.)
Trombone(s) (Tenor) (Tbn.)	Trombone(-i) (tenore(-i)) (Trb.)	Trombone(s) (Trb.)	(Tenor) Posaune(n) (Pos.)
Bass Trombone (B. Tbn.)	Trombone basso (Trb. basso)	Trombone basse (Trb. b.)	Bassposaune B.-Pos.
Baritone(s) or Euphonium(s) (Bar.)	Baritono-(i) (Bar.)	Baritone(s) (Bar.)	Baryton(e) (Bar.)
(Bass) Tuba (Tb.)	Tuba (di bassa) (Tb.)	Tuba (basse) (Tb.)	Tuba or Basstuba (Tb.)
		PERCUSSION	
Timpani or Kettledrums (Timp.)	Timpani (Timp.)	Timbales (Timb.)	Pauken (Pk.)
Bass Drum (B. Dr.)	Gran cassa (Gr. c.)	Grosse Caisse (Gr. C.)	Grosse Trommel (Gr. Tr.)
Snare Drum (S. Dr.)	Tamburo militaire (Tamb.)	Tambour militaire (Tamb.)	Kleine Trommel (Kl. Tr.)
Tenor Drum (T. Dr.)	Tamburo rullante (Tamb. r.)	Caisse roulante Caisse (r.)	Rührtrommel (Rtr.)
Cymbals (Cym.)	Piatti (Ptti.)	Cymbales (Cymb.)	Becken (Beck.)
Suspended Cymbal (Susp. Cym.)	Piatto (sospeso)	Cymbale (suspendue) (Cymb. s.)	Becken (frei)
Antique Cymbals (Ant. Cym.)	Cimbali antichi (Cimb. ant.)	Cymbales antiques (Cymb. ant.)	Antike Zimbeln (Ant. Zimb.)
Finger Cymbals (Fing. Cym.)	————	Crotales (Crot.)	————
Gong (G.)	Tam-tam (Tam.)	Tam-tam (T. T.)	Tam-tam (T.-t.)
Tambourine (Tamb.)	Tamburino (Tamb.)	Tambour de Basque (Tamb. de Basque)	Tamburin (Tamb.)

English	Italian	French	German
	PERCUSSION (cont.)		
Triangle (Trgl.)	Triangolo (Trgl.)	Triangle (Trg.)	Triangel (Trgl.)
Castanets (Casts.)	Castagnette (Cast.)	Castagnettes (Cast.)	Kastagnetten (Kast.)
Chimes or Bells (Tubular)	Campagne (Camp.)	Cloches	Glocken (Glock.)
Glockenspiel or Chime-Bells (Glock.)	Campanelli (Cmplli.)	Carillon or Jeu de Timbres (Car. or J. de T.)	Glockenspiel (Glsp.)
Bongos (Bong.)	Bongos (Bong.)	Bongos (Bong.)	Bongos (Bong.)
Claves	Claves	Claves	Claves
Guiro (Rasper)	Raspe	Râpe	Raspel
Maracas	Maracas	Maracas	Maracas
Rattle (Ratchet)	Raganella	Crécelle	Klapper
Sandpaper Blocks (Sand. Bl.)	Ceppi di carta vetro	Blocs a papier de verre	Sandpapierblocke
Siren	Sirena	Sirène	Sirene
Slapstick (Whip)	Frusta	Fouet	Peitsche
Sleighbells	Sonagli	Grelots	Schelle
Temple Blocks (Temp. Bl.)	————	————	————
Wind Machine	Macchina a venti	Machine à vent	Windmaschine
Wood Block (Wd. Bl.)	Casse li legno	Blocs de bois	Holzkasten
Xylophone (Xyl.)	Xylophono (Xyl.)	Xylophone (Xyl.)	Xylophon (Xyl.)
Vibraphone (Vib.)	Vibrafono (Vibraf.)	Vibraphone (Vibraph.)	Vibraphon (Vibraph.)
Marimba	Marimba	Marimba	Marimba
	HARP AND KEYBOARD		
Harp(s) (Hp.)	Arpa(e) (Arp.)	Harpe(s) (Hrp.)	Harfe(n) (Hrf.)
Celesta (Cel.)	Celesta (Cel.)	Célesta (Cel.)	Celeste (Cel.)
Harpsichord (Hpscd.)	Clavicembalo (Cemb.)	Clavecin (Clav.)	Kielflugel (Kielfl.)
Organ (Org.)	Organo (Org.)	Orgue (Org.)	Orgel (Org.)
Piano (Pn.)	Pianoforte (Pf.)	Piano (Pn.)	Klavier (Klav.)

English	*Italian*	*French*	*German*
		STRINGS	
Violin(s) (Vn.)	Violino(-i) (Vl.)	Violon(s) (Von)	Violine(n) or Geige(n) (Vl.)
Viola (Va.)	Viola(-e) (Va.)	Alto(s) (Alt.)	Bratsche(n) (Br.)
Violoncello(s) or Cello(s) (Vc.)	Violoncello(-i) (Vcl.)	Violoncelle(s) (Vc.)	Violoncello(-e) (Vc.)
Bass(es) or Double bass(es) or Contrabass(es) (B., Db., Cb.)	Contrabasso-(i) (Cb.)	Contrebasse(s) (Cb.)	Kontrabass (bäss) (Kb.)
		VOICES	
Soprano(s) (S.)	Soprano(-i) (S.)	Soprano(s) (S.)	Sopran(e) (S.)
Alto(s) (A.)	Alto(-i) (A.)	Contralto(es) (C.)	Alt(e) (A.)
Tenor(s) (T.)	Tenore(-i) (T.)	Ténor(es) (T.)	Tenor (Tenöre) (T.)
Baritone(s) (Bar.)	Baritono(-i) (Bar.)	Baritone(s) (Bar.)	Baryton(e) (Bar.)
Bass(es) (B.)	Basso(-i) (B.)	Basse(s) (B.)	Bass (Bässe) (B.)

RANGES OF INSTRUMENTS AND VOICES

Instrument	Written Range	Actual Sound
	WOODWINDS	

Piccolo		Octave higher
Flute		As written
Flute in G (Alto flute)		Perfect fourth lower
Oboe		As written
English Horn		Perfect fifth lower
Clarinet in E♭		Minor third higher
Clarinet in B♭		Major second lower
Clarinet in A		Minor third lower

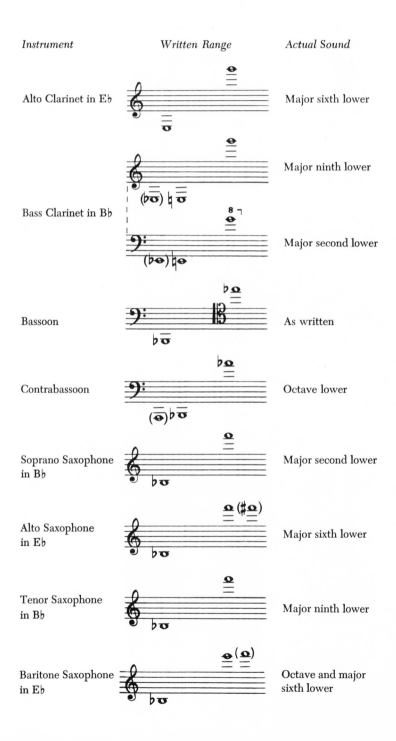

Instrument	Written Range	Actual Sound

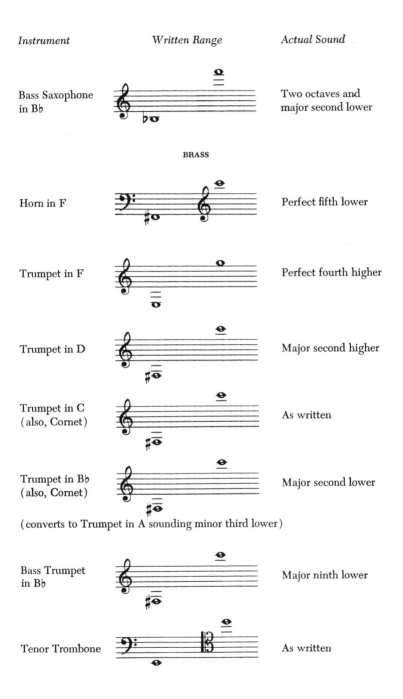

Bass Saxophone in Bb — Two octaves and major second lower

BRASS

Horn in F — Perfect fifth lower

Trumpet in F — Perfect fourth higher

Trumpet in D — Major second higher

Trumpet in C (also, Cornet) — As written

Trumpet in Bb (also, Cornet) — Major second lower

(converts to Trumpet in A sounding minor third lower)

Bass Trumpet in Bb — Major ninth lower

Tenor Trombone — As written

Instrument	Written Range	Actual Sound

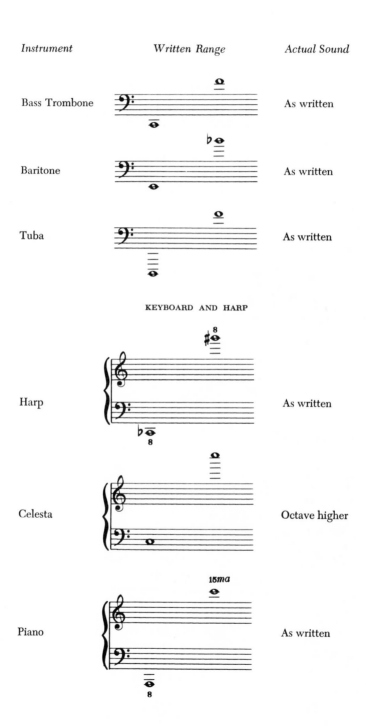

Bass Trombone — As written

Baritone — As written

Tuba — As written

KEYBOARD AND HARP

Harp — As written

Celesta — Octave higher

Piano — As written

Instrument	Written Range	Actual Sound

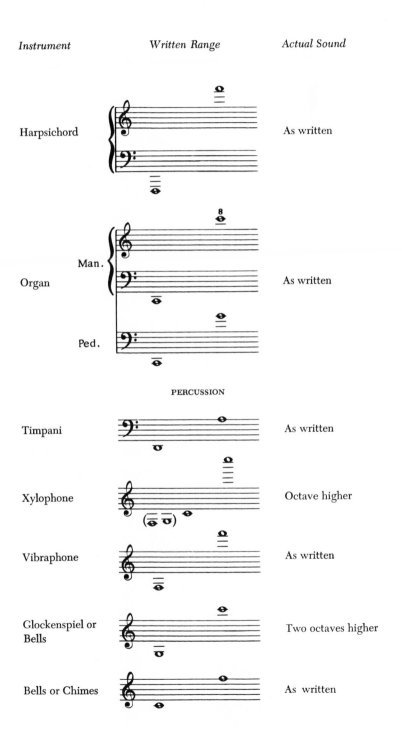

Harpsichord — As written

Organ — Man. / Ped. — As written

PERCUSSION

Timpani — As written

Xylophone — Octave higher

Vibraphone — As written

Glockenspiel or Bells — Two octaves higher

Bells or Chimes — As written

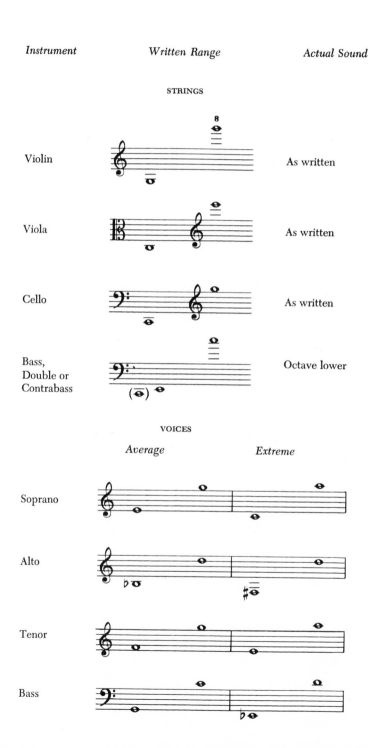

Instrument	Written Range	Actual Sound

STRINGS

Violin — As written

Viola — As written

Cello — As written

Bass, Double or Contrabass — Octave lower

VOICES

Average — Extreme

Soprano

Alto

Tenor

Bass

FREQUENTLY USED DIRECTIONS FOR INSTRUMENTS

English	Italian	French	German
all	tutti	tout	alle
half (section)	la metà	la moitié	die Hälfte
desk or stand	leggio	pupitre	Pult
a2	a2	à2	zu 2
unison	unisono	unis	einfach (or zusammen)
divided	divisi	divisé	geteilt
div. by 3's	div. a 3	div. à 3	dreifach (or zu 3)
div. by 4's	div. a 4	div. à 4	vierfach (or zu 4)
string	corda	corde	Saite
with mute(s)	con sordino(-i)	avec sourdine(s)	mit Dämpfer(n)
remove mute(s)	via sordino(-i)	otez le(s) sourdine(s)	Dämpfer(n) weg
without mute(s)	senza sordino(-i)	sans sourdine(s)	ohne Dämpfer(n)
at the bridge	sul ponticello	sur le chevalet	am Steg
near the sounding board		près de la table	
over the fingerboard	sul tasto	sur la touche	am Griffbrett
at the point of the bow	a punte d'arco	au pointe d'archet	an der Spitze
at the frog	al tallone	au talon	am Frosche
in the ordinary manner	modo ordinario	mode ordinaire	gewöhnlich
harmonic	armonico	harmonique	Flageolett
natural	naturale	naturel	natürlich
open	aperto(-i)	ouvert(s)	offen
stopped	chiuso(-i)	bouché(s)	gestopft
brassy	chiuse	cuivré	schmetternd
hard stick(s)	bachetta(e) di legno	baguette(s) en bois	mit Holzschlägel(n)
soft stick(s)	bachetta(e) di spugna	baguette(s) d'éponge	mit Schwammschlägel(n)
change ____	____ muta in	changez ____	____ nach ____
to ____	____	en ____	umstimmen
bells in the air	campagne in aria	pavillons en l'air	Schalltrichter auf

FOREIGN MUSICAL TERMS

Abandonné (FR.). Free, unrestrained.
Abbandono (IT.). With abandon.
A cappella (IT.). Unaccompanied voices, "for the chapel."
Accelerando (IT.). [Abbr. *accel.*] Gradually faster.
Adagietto (IT.). Faster than adagio.
Adagio (IT.). Slow.
Ad libitum (L.). [Abbr. *ad lib.*] At will, i.e., invented by the performer.
Affettuoso (IT.). Affectionate, tender, warm.
Affrettando (IT.). [Abbr. *affret.*] Hurrying.
Agitato (IT.). Agitated, restless.
Agité (FR.). Agitated.
Al fine (IT.). To the end.
Alla breve (IT.). Implies half-note unit, used with the sign ¢.
Allargando (IT.). [Abbr. *allarg.*] Slowing down, broadening.
Allegretto (IT.). Slower than allegro.
Allegro (IT.). Quick tempo.
Al segno (IT.). To the sign.
Amabile (IT.). Amiable.
Amoroso (IT.). Amorous, tender.
Ancora (IT.). Once more, still.
Andante (IT.). Moderate tempo.
Andantino (IT.). Usually considered as faster than andante.
Anfang (G.). Beginning. *Vom Anfang*, back to the beginning.
Animato (IT.). Animated.
Animé (FR.). Animated.
Anschwellen (G.). Increase, crescendo.
A piacere (IT.). At pleasure, free.
Appassionato (IT.). With passion.
Assai (IT.). Very.
Assez (FR.). Enough, fairly.
A tempo (IT.). Resume tempo.
Attacca (IT.). Go immediately to next section; no pause.
Aussi (FR.). As, also.

Battuta (IT.). Beat; particularly the strong beat of the measure.
Ben (IT.). Well.
Bien (FR.). Very, well.
Brio (IT.). Spirit, vigor.

Calando (IT.). Softer and slower.
Calore (IT.). Warmth.
Cantabile (IT.). Singing style.
Cédez (FR.). Yield, a little slower.
Chaleur (FR.). Warmth.
Coda (IT.). Ending.
Col, coll', colla (IT.). With the; used with other terms.
Come (IT.). As, like.

Comodo, commodo (IT.). Convenient, comfortable tempo.
Con (IT.). With.
Crescendo (IT.). [Abbr. *cresc.*] Increasing in loudness.

Da capo (IT.). [Abbr. D.C.] From the beginning.
Decidé (FR.). Decided.
Deciso (IT.). Decided.
Decrescendo (IT.). [Abbr. *decresc.*] Decreasing in loudness.
Dehors, en dehors (FR.). Outside, from without.
Delicato (IT.). Delicate, soft.
Diminuendo (IT.). [Abbr. *Dim.*] Decreasing in loudness.
Dolce (IT.). Soft and sweet.
Dolcissimo (IT.). Very soft and sweet.
Dolente (IT.). Doleful, sorrowful.
Dolore (IT.). Grief.
Doloroso (IT.). Sorrowful.
Doppio (IT.). Double.
Douce, doux (FR.). Soft, sweet.
Douleur (FR.). Grief, sorrow.
Douloureux (FR.). Sorrowful.

Eilend (G.). Hurrying.
Elan (FR.). Dash.
Elegiaco (IT.). Elegiac.
Enchaînez (FR.). Link, go immediately to next section.
Energico (IT.). Energetic.
Erlöschend (G.). Dying away.
Espressione (IT.). Expression.
Espressivo (IT.). [Abbr. *espress.*] Expressive.
Etwas (G.). Some, somewhat.
Expressif (FR.). Expressive.

Facilement (FR.). Easily.
Feroce (IT.). Ferocious.
Fervore (IT.). Fervor.
Flebile (IT.). Mournful.
Flehend (G.). Imploring.
Flottant (FR.). Floating.
Flüssig (G.). Flowing.
Forte (IT.). Loud, strong.
Fortissimo (IT.). Very loud.
Forza (IT.). Force.
Forzando (IT.). Forcing.
Forzato (IT.). Forced.
Frenetico (IT.). Frenzied.
Freudig (G.). Joyful.
Fröhlich (G.). Cheerful, gay.
Fuoco (IT.). Fire.
Furieux (FR.). Furious.
Furioso (IT.). Furious.

Gai (FR.). Gay.
Gaiment (FR.). Gaily.
Gebunden (G.). Legato.
Gedämpft (G.). Muted.
Gehalten (G.). Sustained.
Gehend (G.). Going along; andante.
Gemächlich (G.). Comfortable; same as comodo.
Gesangvoll (G.). Singing; cantabile.
Getragen (G.). Sustained.
Giocoso (IT.). Playful.
Giusto (IT.). Exact, proper.
Gracieux (FR.). Graceful.
Gradevole (IT.). Pleasing.
Grandioso (IT.). Grand.
Grave (IT.). Grave, slow, solemn.
Grazia (IT.). Grace.
Grazioso (IT.). Graceful.
Gusto (IT.). Taste.

Hurtig (G.). Agile, quick.

Immer (G.). Always, ever.
Indeciso (IT.). Undecided.
Innig (G.). Heartfelt, fervent.
Intrepido (IT.). Intrepid, bold.
Istesso tempo (IT.). The same tempo.

Klagend (G.). Lamenting.
Klang (G.). Sound, sonority.
Klangfarbe (G.). Tonecolor.

Langsam (G.). Slow.
Largamente (IT.). Broadly.
Largo (IT.). Slow and broad.
Larghetto (IT.). Less slow or broad than largo.
Lebhaft (G.). Lively.
Legato (IT.). Smooth.
Légèrement (FR.). Lightly.
Leggiero (IT.). [Abbr. *legg.*] Light.
Lent (FR.). Slow.
Lento (IT.). Slow.
Licenza (IT.). Liberty.
Lieblich (G.). Charming, sweet.
L'istesso tempo (IT.). Same tempo.
Lo stesso tempo (IT.). Same tempo.
Lourd (FR.). Heavy.
Lusingando (IT.). Coaxing, flattering.
Lustig (G.). Merry, gay.

Maestoso (IT.). Majestic.
Marcato (IT.). Marked.
Marziale (IT.). Martial, marchlike.
Mässig (G.). Moderate.
Meno (IT.). Less.
Mesto (IT.). Sad.
Mezzo (IT.). Half.
Moderato (IT.). Moderate.
Modéré (FR.). Moderate.
Molto (IT.). Very.
Morbido (IT.). Smooth.
Morendo (IT.). Dying away.
Mosso (IT.). Moved.
Moto (IT.). Motion.

Nicht (G.). Not.
Non (IT.). Not.
Non tanto (IT.). Not so much.
Non troppo (IT.). Not too much.

Ossia (IT.). Or, otherwise. An alternate or easier version.

Parlando (IT.). As if spoken.
Perdendo (si) (IT.). Dying away.
Pesante (IT.). Heavy, ponderous.
Peu (FR.). Little.
Piacevole (IT.). Agreeable, pleasing.
Piano (IT.). Soft.
Pianissimo (IT.). Very soft.
Pieno (IT.). Full.
Piu (IT.). More.
Plus (FR.). More.
Poco (IT.). Little.
Poi (IT.). Then, after.
Pomposo (IT.). Pompous, stately.
Pressez (FR.). Accelerate.
Prestissimo (IT.). Extremely fast.
Presto (IT.). Very fast.
Primo (IT.). First.

Quasi (IT.). Almost, as if.

Rallentando (IT.). [Abbr. *rall.*] Slowing the tempo.
Religioso (IT.). Religious in manner.
Renforcer (FR.). Reinforce, increase.
Retenant (FR.). Holding back.
Rinforzando (IT). [Abbr. *rinf., rfz.*] Reinforcing.
Risoluto (IT.). Boldly, resolutely.
Ritardando (IT.). [Abbr. *ritard., rit.*] Slowing the tempo.

Ritenuto (IT.). [Abbr. *rit.*] Slowing the tempo, actually immediate slowing.
Rubato (IT.). Robbed; flexible tempo.
Ruhig (G.). Quiet.

Scherzando (IT.). Playful.
Schleppend (G.). Dragging.
Schnell (G.). Quick.
Schwindend (G.). Dying away.
Secco (IT.). Dry.
Secondo (IT.). Second.
Segue (IT.). Follows; continue or proceed.
Sehr (G.). Very.
Semplice (IT.). Simple.
Sempre (IT.). Always.
Sereno (IT.). Serene.
Sforzando, sforzato (IT.). [Abbr. *sf., sfz.*] Forced, forcing.
Simile (IT.). Similar, continue.
Slentando (IT.). Gradually slower.
Smorzando (IT.). [Abbr. *smorz.*] Dying away.
Solennel (FR.). Solemn.
Sospirando (IT.). Sighing.
Sostenuto (IT.). [Abbr. *sost.*] Sustained.
Sotto (IT.). Under.
Soupirant (FR.). Sighing.
Soutenu (FR.). Sustained.
Spianato (IT.). Even, smooth.
Spiritoso (IT.). Spirited.
Stentando (IT.). Laboring, holding back.
Sterbend (G.). Dying away.
Strepitoso (IT.). Noisy.
Stretto (IT.). Contracted; also suddenly faster. In a fugue, overlapping of entries.
Stringendo (IT.). [Abbr. *string.*] Becoming faster.
Subito (IT.). Suddenly.
Suivez (FR.). Follow.

Tacet (L.). Is silent.
Tanto (IT.). So much.
Teneramente (IT.). Tenderly.
Tenuto (IT.). [Abbr. *Ten.*] Hold to full value.
Tranquillo (IT.). Tranquil, calm.
Trattenuto (IT.). [Abbr. *tratt.*] Held back.
Traurig (G.). Sad.
Très (FR.). Very.
Troppo (IT.). Too much.

Un peu (FR.). A little.
Unruhig (G.). Restless.

Veloce (IT.). Fast.
Vif (FR.). Lively.

Vigoroso (IT.). Vigorous.
Vigoureux (FR.). Vigorous.
Vite (FR.). Quick.
Vivace (IT.). Vivacious, lively.
Vivo (IT.). Lively.

Wachsend (G.). Increasing in loudness.
Wuchtig (G.). Forceful, heavy.

Zart (G.). Tender.
Zeitmass (G.). Tempo.
Ziemlich (G.). Rather.

INDEX

INDE

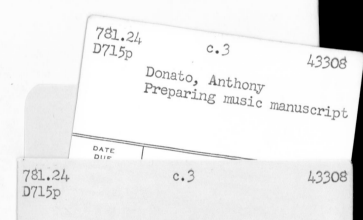

INDEX OF MUSICAL SYMBOLS

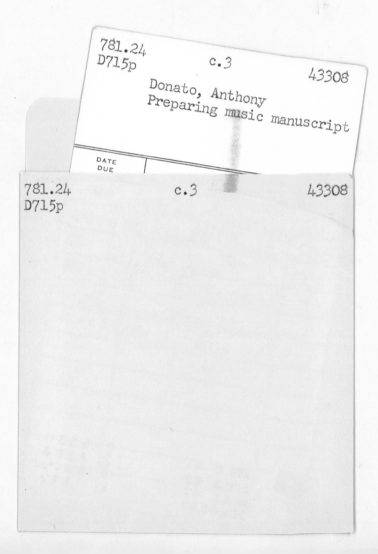